THE MUSIC PERFORMANCE LIBRARY

A PRACTICAL GUIDE FOR ORCHESTRA, BAND, AND OPERA LIBRARIANS

RUSS GIRSBERGER
and LAURIE LAKE

Published by
Meredith Music Publications
a division of G.W. Music, Inc.
4899 Lerch Creek Ct., Galesville, MD 20765
http://www.meredithmusic.com

Cover photo and design: Russ and Shawn Girsberger

International Standard Book Number: 978-1-57463-166-1
Cataloging-in-Publication Data is on file with the Library of Congress.
Library of Congress Control Number: 2011929834
Printed and bound in U.S.A.

DEDICATION

My sincere thanks to my mentors who taught me so much about this profession: Mike Ressler, Frank Byrne, Marty Burlingame, John Perkel, Larry Tarlow, and Bob Sutherland.

And to my teachers who let me run my first libraries: Michael Warner and Robert Spevacek.

And to my wife, Shawn, who always makes me and my work look good.

Russ Girsberger
Warwick, New York

CONTENTS

Preface vii

Chapter 1 **Library Basics** 1

    Your First Day in a New Library 2

    How to Prepare a Program From Scratch. 6

    Library Etiquette 10

    Library Supplies and Equipment 12

Chapter 2 **Acquisitions** 19

    Purchasing Music. 20

    Renting Music 22

    Other Sources for Acquiring Music 25

    Acquisitions Record Keeping. 28

    Receiving Music—Purchases 30

    Receiving Music—Rentals 31

    Acquisitions checklist 32

Chapter 3 **Cataloging** 33

    Creating Your Library Catalog 34

    Cataloging Authorities 37

    Resources for Cataloging 40

    Score Identification 44

    Shelf Arrangement and Filing Systems 52

    Subject Access to the Performance Library
        Catalog 55

    Cataloging checklist 59

Chapter 4 **Processing** **61**

    Score Order. 62

    Property Markings. 66

    Numbering Parts 67

    Inventory Records 70

    The Performance Record. 71

    Creating a Preservation Set. 72

    Processing checklist 74

Chapter 5 **Music Preparation** **75**

    How to Mark Parts. 76

    Divisi Markings 81

    Performance Aids for the Player 85

    Cuts. 86

    Rehearsal Figures 88

    Music Notation Guidelines 93

    Binding Music for Performance 99

    Fixing Page Turns 103

    Making Copies 109

    Copying March Parts for Concert Use 110

    Music Preparation checklist 114

Chapter 6 **Rehearsal and Performance** **117**

    Booking Parts into Folders 118

    Concert Duty Procedure 119

    Collecting Parts. 122

    Breaking Down Folders 123

    Returning Rental Music 124

    Putting Away Concert Music 126

    Rehearsal and Performance checklist 127

Chapter 7 **Additional Responsibilities** **129**

What to Tell Student Composers. 130

What to Tell Student Conductors. 137

Preparing Audition Lists 142

Preparing Digital Audition Excerpts 146

Errata 150

Suggestions for Completing Errata Forms 154

Band Instrument Substitutions. 160

Appendix A **Library Forms** **161**

Appendix B **Glossary** **175**

Appendix C **Bibliography**. **181**

Index 191

About the Authors. 196

PREFACE

This book was developed from educational materials created for student workers in the performance libraries at New England Conservatory and The Juilliard School. I wrote a series of handouts and checklists that explained performance library work in more detail and found that the students appreciated the training and the extra responsibility. It also helped them understand the administrative operation of their ensembles and made them more aware of the library's value to performers. Consequently, the bow markings they copied began to make sense musically and the errata they fixed contributed to a more accurate performance. I was also proud to see that several of these students took occasional jobs as performance librarians, putting their education to work, and that a few of the best went on to become professional librarians in other ensembles.

To date there is no college curriculum where you can learn to become a performance librarian, but my friend and colleague Laurie Lake had made great strides toward establishing such a goal, first at Indiana University, and then with her summer internship program at the Interlochen Center for the Arts. She was the logical person to help develop a programmed approach to teach the many facets of performance librarianship.

I have also been privileged to learn from many exceptional librarians, in person and through the Major Orchestra Librarians' Association, the professional organization for performance librarians. MOLA members are generous with their time and information and it was in this spirit that I wanted to share some of this knowledge. This led to creating a book that I would have wanted to read when I was starting my career.

The checklists, essays, and step-by-step instructions are intended for those who want to learn the basic procedures of performance library work. They will be helpful to student librarians and community ensemble librarians who are just starting out, as well as conductors and music directors who want to train their own library staff.

Russ Girsberger
Warwick, New York

Like most of us who have served in this profession at one time or another, I accidentally fell into the position of orchestra librarian. It was in a small community ensemble in a medium-sized town in a very large western state. I'm not too proud to say that I got the gig because no one else would do it. This started my slow side down the slippery slope into librarianship. To say I wish I knew then what I know now, particularly after assisting Russ assemble this tome, is an understatement. My hope is that this book provides guidance to someone who is new to the profession and unaware that there is anyone else in the world crazy enough to do this for a living. Ensemble librarians do exist in hidden corners in the universe.

Laurie Lake
Cleveland, Ohio

1

LIBRARY
BASICS

Your First Day in a New Library

or How to put your library in order and what to do next

You have just started a new job and walked into your new library on your first day of work. Soon you will be expected to order and prepare music, but first you need to determine what you already have and how to find it. The library collection itself may look tidy and well-organized or it may be a mess. What do you do to find your way and start using the resources you have available? Here are some steps to help you get control of your music collection in the short-term and the long-term.

1. Determine if there is a catalog for the collection, in any format: index cards, computer database (electronic or printout), or even a handwritten ledger.

   a) If there is an accurate catalog, this will be how you gain access to the collection.
   b) If there is no catalog, move to step 2.

2. Determine the arrangement of the music on the shelves or in the files.

   a) Is it:

      - alphabetical by composer or title?
      - by accession number?
      - by another numerical or alpha-numeric system?
      - by genre (pops, solos, overtures, etc.)?
      - lying in a pile in the center of the room?

   b) Is there music for more than one type of ensemble?

      - orchestra
      - band
      - chorus
      - jazz ensemble
      - chamber ensemble

   c) If so:

      - is the music for each ensemble shelved separately?
      - do they each have their own numerical or alpha-numeric system?
      - do they each have their own catalog?

If you have an accurate catalog and your music is arranged in a functional order, then most of your work is done and you can move forward using your collection.

If you don't have a catalog, but can discern an order to the collection, you can still get access to the music with just a little extra hunting.

If you don't have a catalog and you can't figure out how the music is arranged, then you have your work cut out for you.

The following steps will help restore or impose order on your library

Apply them as needed, depending on the condition of your library, to help get control of your music collection.

1. Group your music together by ensemble.
2. Group your music by the general physical size of the parts within that ensemble. This will help maximize the storage space you have available, so that oversize items are not crammed into a small space and small items are not lost when interfiled with larger items. This can be applied a couple of ways, depending on your holdings. If you have:

    a) Band music: Separate the small march-size music (usually printed on 7 × 5¼ inch paper) from the larger size "concert" music. March music can be stored in smaller envelopes for easier access and better protection of the paper. However, marches in modern concert-size editions and those that have been enlarged for concert use should be shelved with the concert music.

    b) Choral music: Separate the thick, bound scores for oratorios, masses, and other large-scale compositions from the standard-sized choral octavos. The bound parts take up a lot of shelf space and these works are usually not performed frequently. To gain more room in your library, these scores can be stored offsite or in a satellite storage area and reclaimed when needed.

    c) Special collections: These are items unique to your holdings that you will want to store apart from your working collection because of their condition or significance. This can include early or rare editions, original compositions or arrangements in manuscript, sets marked for use by your resident conductor or music director, or music associated with a notable performer or donor (e.g., the Aaron Copland collection or the Vaughn Monroe collection). This music may require extra care and special housing, such as acid-free boxes and envelopes, and it is easier to protect if shelved by itself.

3. Once your music is in functional groups, determine how best to arrange it on your storage shelves or cabinets. This may be determined, in part, by the storage space you have available. Is it open shelving, closed cabinets, or file drawers? Do you have one library area, or will the collection be spread across more than one room or building?

    There are several ways to arrange your music, for example:

    a) By accession number. Each work or set of parts is given a unique number in sequence (1, 2, 3, 4, etc.). New works are given the next number in the sequence. This system works well for large collections as it maximizes your storage space and avoids shifting sets to maintain the order. A database or card file is used to provide access to specific works.

b) Alphabetically by composer, then by title. This arrangement is fairly easy to use and convenient if your conductors prefer to browse the collection when deciding on a program. Be sure to allow enough room to interfile new acquisitions throughout the collection or be prepared to shift sets around to maintain the alphabetical order.

c) By genre (overtures, marches, pops, symphonies). This arrangement may also help conductors who like to browse the collection looking for programming ideas.

Remember that a database catalog can be configured to search, sort, and print reports of the holdings by any alphabetical or genre criteria.

4. Decide how to store the scores. These can be housed with the parts or shelved separately by themselves. If your conductors or players have access to the scores for study and perusal, then storing them separately on shelves will allow easier access without the need to dig into each set of parts. You will also need a storage area for scores without accompanying sets, such as rental works or editions not in your collection.

   If you store the scores separately from the parts, you should also plan to group them by size—miniature scores shelved apart from large scores—so that the smaller items are not damaged or misplaced if interfiled with the larger ones.

5. Select and acquire the proper supplies to house your music: cabinets, folders, envelopes, labels, inventory sheets, etc. See the article on "Library Supplies and Equipment" for more information on this step.

6. Create a catalog of your holdings. See the chapter on "Cataloging" to help decide what type of catalog to use and the steps to determine and enter the data.

7. When time allows, do a wall-to-wall inventory of your library. This can be a long, time-consuming process, but it is the best way to see the state of your collection first hand. As you examine each set of parts:

   a) Prepare accurate inventory forms that will remain with the music. (See the Appendix for examples of inventory forms.)

   b) Confirm and update the information in your library catalog.

   c) Make a note of the completeness and condition of the music.

Now that your music collection is in order, you can continue with the rest of the library:

8. Order supplies for your day-to-day library work (pencils, erasers, etc.). See the article on "Library Supplies and Equipment" for a complete list.

9. Arrange workstations to allow room for building folders/breaking down folders, bowing and editing parts, etc.

10. Arrange areas for storing and distributing the concert music and folders.
11. Prepare forms and files for your daily activities: acquisitions, budget, cataloging, processing, distribution, and program preparation. Examples of library forms can be found in the Appendix. Keep a clean master copy of each form in electronic format (a word processor or PDF file) or in a file folder or notebook so that you can run new copies from a first generation original.

How to Prepare a Program From Scratch

You are a new librarian in your first job. Your conductor has just handed you the first program of the fall season. What do you do now?

First:

See which pieces you already have in your library. Pull them off the shelf and examine them for:

1. Completeness

    a) Are all the wind parts there?
    b) Do you have enough string parts for each section?

2. Condition

    a) Do the parts need repair (taping, binding, torn corners, etc.)?
    b) Or are they so old and tattered that they must be replaced?

3. Edition

    a) Do you have more than one edition?[1]
    b) Make sure the editions are not mixed together.

4. Rehearsal figures

    a) Are there rehearsal numbers, letters, and/or measure numbers?
    b) Make note of this information and ensure that the conductor's score is from the same publisher and has the same rehearsal figures.

5. Performance history

    a) Can you tell when the set was last used and who conducted the performance?
    b) What is the source of the bowings?

Always check your library holdings first, even if the work is available only on rental. You may have a set of parts in the collection that is:

---

1 What is an "edition"? In short, an edition is usually one set of parts from a given publisher (such as a Breitkopf & Härtel set or a Bärenreiter set), or differing sets from the same publisher (such as a 1905 Breitkopf & Härtel Leipzig set or a 1965 Breitkopf & Härtel Wiesbaden set). These editions may differ in several ways, mostly in what musical choices the editor has made. When comparing editions, look for differences in the markings (slurs and articulations), in the layout of the music on the page (different page turns, rehearsal letters versus measure numbers), and in the publication information (different plate numbers or publisher catalog numbers).

1. An on-deposit rental set, housed in your library, usually with your orchestra's bowings and markings from a previous performance. If so:

   a) Place a rental order for this music so that the appropriate fees are paid to the publisher.
   b) Tell the publisher that you will use your on-deposit set so they don't send you another set of parts.

2. Music that was previously available for purchase but now is rental only. This can include:

   a) Reprint editions that were returned to copyright protection under the GATT Treaty (General Agreement on Tariffs and Trade) in 1994. This includes many works by 20th-century Russian composers (Shostakovich, Prokofiev, Glière, Glinka, etc.) previously sold by Kalmus, Luck's Music, Broude Brothers, or other reprint publishers. If you own these sets, you may perform from your parts without paying a rental fee, although you must still pay the performing rights fee to the appropriate organization (ASCAP, BMI, SESAC, etc.).
   b) Other works which were once for sale, such as *Rhapsody in Blue, An American in Paris, Second Essay for Orchestra*, or others.

Second:

For those works that you do not have in your library, you must determine which are available for sale and which are available only on a rental basis, and a source for each.

The date of a composition may help determine if a work is for sale or rent. In the United States, the duration of copyright protection varies depending on the creator (individual or corporate entity) and the date of creation. A rule of thumb, at the time of this writing, is that works composed or published in 1922 or earlier are in the public domain.[2] In turn, most music composed or published in 1923 or later is protected under the copyright law of the United States from unauthorized reproduction, so these works are most likely available only from the publisher. (If you have a question about copyright, it is best to visit a website that specializes in copyright information for your country, or even consult a copyright specialist.) Due to the cost to engrave, print, and distribute works for large ensembles, most publishers will rent this music on a per-performance basis because they will make more money than if they sold the work outright. There are some exceptions to this rule of thumb, so it is worthwhile to check the publisher's website or ask your music dealer if you are uncertain about the availability of a specific work.

---

2   What is the "public domain"? Works in the public domain are no longer protected by the copyright law and as such may be reproduced, edited, or arranged without the approval of, or payment to, the copyright holder. These works may be re-purposed or redistributed by anyone. This is one way that reprint publishers find music to reproduce and sell under their imprint.

If the music is rental: You are usually limited to ordering from the publisher who holds the copyright or performing rights for that work. Contact the rental library of the publisher and place an order for the music.

For example, let's say that the last work on your concert program is Béla Bartók's Concerto for Orchestra. First, check David Daniels's book[3] or website. This resource lists many standard repertoire works and includes information about instrumentation, duration, and publisher. Looking in the Daniels, you see that the publisher of this work is Boosey & Hawkes. There are no other publishers listed, so Boosey is the sole source. Visit the Boosey & Hawkes website (www.Boosey.com) to learn that the work is available on a rental (or "hire") basis only. Follow the links to the rental department page and fill out a rental request form to order the music. If your organization has established an account with Boosey, proceed with your order. If you need to establish an account, follow the appropriate links to set one up. If you aren't certain whether or not your organization has an account, call the rental library and ask. You will need to know your account number to place an order.

If the music is for sale: Let's say that the second work on your concert is Mozart's Piano Concerto No. 20, K. 466. Looking in the Daniels, you see four publishers:

Bärenreiter   *Breitkopf*   *Kalmus*   *Luck's*

Each publisher's edition will have essentially the same musical notes for this familiar work. The differences can be seen in the editor's interpretation of Mozart's articulations and style, as well as the appearance and layout of the music on the page (i.e., the size of the staves and note heads, accommodation of page turns, size and texture of the paper, etc.).

Two of the publishers on the list (Kalmus, Luck's) are reprint publishers.[4] Both of these publishers sell sets reproduced from the same early Breitkopf & Härtel edition. The Bärenreiter publication is identified as an "urtext" edition, edited by Engel and Heussner. The Breitkopf edition is probably a more modern edition or printing of their early edition. You can find out more about each edition from the publisher's website, which is listed in the appendix of the Daniels, or found using an Internet search engine.

---

3   David Daniels, *Orchestral Music: A Handbook* (4th ed. Lanham, Md.: Scarecrow Press, 2005). An online version is available by subscription at http://www.orchestralmusic.com.

4   What are "reprint publishers"? These are companies that publish editions of music that are in the public domain or no longer protected by the copyright law. They reproduce these editions, replacing the original publisher's name with their own, and sell the music. These printings may vary in quality (darkness of printing, size of notes, legibility). Most are direct reproductions from the original source, warts and all (errata, bad page turns, etc.), although some companies offer corrected editions or individual transposed parts for these standard works. In the United States, the largest reprint publishers are Broude Brothers Limited, Edwin F. Kalmus & Company, Luck's Music Library, Subito Music, and Dover Publications (for scores only).

To order music that is available for sale, it is easiest to work with a reputable music dealer. A dealer can provide one-stop shopping by placing orders from several publishers, coordinating deliveries, and consolidating shipping and billing for you. The best dealers can also provide information about publishers, editions, pricing, and delivery options. These customer service features may come free of charge, but if you consult a dealer for this information you should also place your orders with them to encourage their continued good service.

Before you acquire any of these editions, it is most important to first ask your conductor, "Maestro, which score will you be using for this work." Your conductor may prefer one edition over another and you should acquire performance materials that match. Make sure that the conductor's score and the ensemble's parts have the same rehearsal figures and performance markings in order to save time and confusion in rehearsal.

The next steps

Now that you have identified and located your music, you can acquire it. See the articles on "Renting Music" and "Purchasing Music" for specific details on each of those procedures. The article on "Acquisitions Record Keeping" will explain how to document and track your orders and expenses.

Next read the articles on "Receiving Music" (purchases and rentals) to learn how to check in the music you have ordered.

If you have purchased the music, the chapter on "Cataloging" will tell how to identify and record the music in your library catalog. The chapter on "Processing" will show the steps to arrange, number, file, and store your music.

Regardless if the music is purchased or rented, if it will be used on an upcoming performance, read the chapter on "Music Preparation" to learn the steps to make the parts ready for the players.

Finally, read the chapter on "Rehearsal and Performance" for instructions on distributing, collecting, and returning or reshelving the music both before and after the concert.

Library Etiquette

'°ve had the good fortune to work with a number of college students and young adults over the years. Below, you will find some of the major points regarding professionalism and customer service in the workplace that these young librarians have found helpful. I find they always bear repeating.

1. **Be prepared.**
   Enough said.

2. **Be on time.**
   It's not a good idea to come blowing into the library five minutes before a rehearsal begins. Just because others in the group may do so, does not make it okay for you, unless this is how you would like to be perceived by your colleagues.

3. **Know your stuff and be good at it.**
   Remember, you are providing a service.

4. **Listen.**
5. **Create and pay into a savings account of goodwill.**

A genuine smile takes two seconds and will reap benefits for years. Listen to concerts. Appreciate and respect your colleagues, both inside and outside the library. Show an interest in what is going on around you musically. Learn the musicians' names and know which part they play.

Ask the horn player if the voicing makes sense. Invite a string player to check out an unclear marking. Tell the clarinetist you loved their solo. This can all be done in a way as to not be a pushover, but simply to show your colleagues that you appreciate their knowledge and ability. Plus, you might learn a thing or two about an unfamiliar instrument.

This is not to say that you will leap at every request immediately, although some, by their nature, require instant attention. By showing you care for your work and are aware of your part in the whole operation, you will gain the respect of your colleagues.

Accept the fact that somewhere along the way, you will make a mistake. You will need the understanding of your colleagues while you correct the error. If you've isolated yourself in the library and made little effort to interact with your fellow musicians, the chances of the mistake remaining a minor ripple are non-existent. These are the times that you can make a withdrawal from the account of goodwill into which you've been paying.

The library is not the center of the world. It is part of a larger organization that may have its own dysfunction, but your role is to contribute in a helpful, positive manner. Everyone has their own problems. The number of hours you will need to tackle a stack of bowings does not translate into a major catastrophe for others, nor do they want to hear about it. Remember, you are, hopefully, doing this because you obtain something in the process that you cannot achieve anywhere else in your life. Enjoy the experience and continue to grow.

Also, remember the workplace is not a democracy. There are those whose verdicts weigh much more heavily than others. If you're looking for equal rights, join a political action group.

We're all human beings doing the best that we can do. Sometimes someone else's best is not your best, but the shoe could just as easily be worn on the other foot.

Resources

Covey, Stephen R. *The Seven Habits of Highly Effective People.* New York: Free Press, 2004.

> The seminal text on developing solid character and increasing respect for both oneself and others.

Carlaw, Peggy, and Vasudha Kathleen Deming. *The Big Book of Customer Service Training Games.* Maidenhead, N.J.: McGraw-Hill Professional, 2006.

> A smorgasbord of games to play one-on-one or in groups to increase awareness of perceptions from the customer's viewpoint.

Manager Tools LLC. "Become a more effective manager and leader/Manager Tools." http://www.manager-tools.com.

> A thorough collection of podcasts covering everything from acing a job interview to dealing with a difficult boss.

Library Supplies and Equipment

The right supplies not only help produce a better quality product, they make the job go easier. Most of these items are found in library, office, stationery, or craft and scrapbooking supply stores. These supplies were recommended by members of the Major Orchestra Librarians' Association (MOLA).

Bowing pencils

Pencils can be a personal item because their size and weight determine how comfortable they feel in your hand. Choose a soft graphite pencil that makes a dark mark which can easily be erased in case the player needs to change a bowing on the stand. Avoid pencils that are either so soft that their marks smear when the page is rubbed, or so hard that the pencil tip creases or pokes through the paper.

Most of these recommended pencils can be found at stationery stores or through online dealers.

- Papermate Mirado Black Warrior No. 2 (HB2) [formerly Berol 350]
- Dixon Ticonderoga Wood Pencils, Extra Soft No. 1 (#13881)
- Dixon Tri-Conderoga HB2 (three-sided pencil)
- Sanford Draughting #02237(314)
- Staedtler Mars Lumograph 100 model (2B or 3B)
- Pentel QE409 automatic pencil with 0.9mm 2B lead
- Pentel QE519 "Twist-Erase" automatic pencil with 0.9mm 2B lead
- Koh-I-Noor Rapidomatic mechanical draughting pencil (#5639), with 0.9mm 2B lead
- Magic Writer Pencils (available only from Pacific Music Papers, Reseda, CA, phone: 818-343-4223)

Occasionally colored pencils (usually red or blue) can be used to help indicate mute changes, instrument changes, or other notable events in the music. They should never be used to mark bowings and should not be overused so that they lose their effectiveness. Autopoint, Inc. makes the Twinpoint, a mechanical pencil with both red and blue lead (http://www.autopointinc.com).

For more information, fans of pencils and other writing implements often post detailed and personal reviews on these websites:

http://davesmechanicalpencils.blogspot.com

http://www.penciltalk.org

http://www.pencilrevolution.com

Erasers

Choose an eraser that will remove pencil markings completely and not leave residue embedded in the paper. Drafting and mechanical drawing erasers work well. Some are available in pen-shaped "clickable" models.

- Staedtler Mars White Plastic Eraser (#526 50)
- Sanford Magic Rub Eraser (#1954)
- Papermate Pink Pearl (#70520) and White Pearl (#70626) erasers
- Tombow Mono plastic eraser (available in different sizes)

Electric erasers are helpful when working with fragile and delicate paper or for bulk erasing many parts. Most manufacturers offer standard and cordless models. Some popular brands are Bruning, Koh-I-Nor, Staedtler Mars, Alvin, and Sakura.

Rulers

A small ruler is handy for drawing straight lines in music notation (crescendos, diminuendos, bar lines, note stem lines, etc.). There are many brands of rulers, but a good choice is the C-Thru brand graphic ruler. It allows you to see through to the music you are marking and the beveled edge won't allow ink pens to smear: #B-50, 1 × 6 inches long; #B-60, 1 × 12 inches long.

Drafting templates with circles and boxes are helpful to mark rehearsal figures and other edits. Some models in a convenient size include:

- Pickett General Purpose Jr. template (#10851)
- Pickett Inking template (#10431)
- Rapidesign Pocket Pal Template (#R-50)
- Rapidesign Sketch Mate (#R-19)

Pens

Wide tip and fine tip pens can be used when making permanent fixes or additions to the parts, including correcting errata and marking rehearsal figures or measure numbers.

- Papermate Flair felt tip (also available in Ultra Fine tip)
- Sanford Uniball (in both Micro and Deluxe Micro tip widths)
- Sanford Uniball Jetstream 0.7mm fine point
- Pigma Micron (acid-free ink pens in six tip widths)
- Staedtler Pigment Liner (available in nine tip widths)
- Pilot Precise V5 and V7 Rolling Ball
- Bic Accountant Fine Point ink pen

Correction tape and fluid

Correction tape is used to correct errata in the parts. It goes on dry and can be written over immediately. There are several different models in a variety of sizes and shapes. Some manufacturers make refillable models.

- Liquid Paper DryLine
- Bic Wite-Out
- Tombow Mono
- Pentel Presto!

Each of these companies also makes correction fluid in a variety of colors, some of which match cream-colored paper (for example, Bic Wite-Out in Buff). Correction fluid pens can be used for small spot fixes and detailed corrections.

Adhesives

These products are helpful for cut-and-paste projects or to affix inserts in parts.

- Avery Glue Stic, available as permanent or removable
- Tombow Mono Adhesive, available as permanent or removable, in a handy rolling dispenser
- Sanford Liquid Paper Dryline Adhesive
- 3M Spray Mount Artist's Adhesive

Bowing boxes

If you have section leaders, students, or volunteers who do bowmarking for the library, a convenient way to help them do their work is to provide a bowing box that contains all the supplies necessary to mark their parts.

The box which holds all these items can be a simple pencil case from a school supply or office supply company. Plastic boxes may be more resilient than cardboard, but should be large enough to hold all the supplies that may be useful: pencils, eraser, ruler, correction tape, pens, etc.

A folder to carry the parts and the box will help protect them from loss and damage. An example is:

- Smead Redrope Expanding Wallet, extra wide legal size (no. 71166).

In addition to the bowing and writing supplies mentioned above, the following items are essential supplies in any performance library.

Adhesive tape

Standard office adhesive tape should be non-yellowing and permanent.

- 3M Scotch 810 Magic Tape

Temporary tape can be used for inserts or cuts that need to be removed after the performance.

- 3M Scotch 811 Magic Removable Tape

For fragile documents that need to be preserved (not used for performance), use acid-free, preservation-quality paper tape, available from most library supply companies (Gaylord, Neschen, Demco, Brodart, etc.).

- Neschen Filmoplast paper tape (www.neschen.com)
- Lineco document repair tape
- Lineco Japanese hinge tape

Binding tape

This is used to attach individual pages together so they make a single part or booklet. The tape should be long-lasting and flexible to allow the pages to lay flat on the stand and hold up to repeated use. MOLA librarians recommend:

- VPC Music Master Binding System (www.vpcinc.com)
- Kapco Easy Bind Repair Tape (www.kapco.com)
- 3M Scotch 888 Conservation and Preservation Tape (www.3M.com)
- 3M Micropore and Durapore Surgical Tape (www.3M.com)
- Tape Rite "Crystal Clear" (www.tape-rite.com)
- Neschen Filmoplast binding tapes (www.neschen.com)

Hinge tape is made by library and archival supply companies, including:

- Gaylord Bros. (http://www.gaylord.com)
- University Products (http://www.universityproducts.com)
- Gamble Music Company (http://www.gamblemusic.com)

Binding supplies

Bookbinder needles, glue, brushes, and bone folders are sold by library and archival supply companies:

- Gaylord Bros. (http://www.gaylord.com)
- University Products (http://www.universityproducts.com)
- Brodart Company (http://www.shopbrodart.com)

Saddle or booklet staplers are manufactured by office supply companies, such as:

- Bostitch (http://www.bostitch.com)
- Swingline (http://www.acco.com/swingline)
- Staplex (http://www.staplex.com)
- ISP Stitching and Bindery Products (http://www.ispstitching.com)

Coil and comb binding machines

For large scores and parts with many pages, an edge binding system is necessary. Many librarians prefer the coil spiral binding over the comb binding because of durability, flexibility, and quieter page turns. Several companies make these binders, but look for machines with an "open throat" that allows large scores to be bound on their entire length.

- Plastikoil (www.plastikoil.com)
- Southwest Plastic Binding Company (www.swplastic.com)
- Akiles CoilMac (www.akiles.com)

These and other brands may be purchased directly from the manufacturer or from authorized dealers, such as MyBinding.com or BindingMachine.com.

Photocopy paper

To create performance quality parts, use a paper of a heavy weight that will stand upright on the music stand and of suitable opacity that printing from the opposite side will not bleed through. A 60 or 70 lb. offset paper works well and can be purchased from paper distributors or printers in common sizes (11 × 17 inches, 10 × 13 inches, 12 × 9 inches, or similar proportions as your photocopier will allow).

Many libraries and publishers use a light cream or ivory-colored paper that doesn't reflect the bright lights of the stage. Insist on smooth or uncoated paper without a surface texture.

Music storage supplies

For storage of music on the shelf, the choices are wide-ranging and based, in part, on cost and practicality for each library. Ideally, the music would be stored flat on a shelf, not on its edge, and be protected from light, both sunlight and fluorescent light. Some possibilities for music storage include:

Envelopes. Large catalog envelopes, measuring approximately 12 × 15 inches, are available from office supply stores (Staples, OfficeMax, etc.) or from shipping supply companies (Uline). Large archival envelopes, in a variety of sizes, offer better long-term protection for the music and are available from library and preservation supply companies (Gaylord, Highsmith, Hollinger Metal Edge, Conservation Resources International).

Expandable wallet folders may also be used. They come in several different sizes that can accommodate a variety of parts. Available from office supply stores, an example is the Smead Redrope Expanding Wallet, extra wide legal size (no. 71166).

Boxes. A few companies make sturdy, cardboard, music storage boxes, measuring approximately 11½ × 15 × 3½ inches. These take up more space on the shelf, but provide extra protection for the music. They are available from Gaylord (item no. MA-990) and Gamble Music Company (item no. 70-BMSB and 70-MSB1).

Archival-quality boxes in a variety of sizes may also be used, available from the same companies as the archival envelopes (see above).

Specialty music products. Music supply companies also make envelopes and boxes designed specifically for sheet music. Some have pre-printed part inventories on the outside for convenience. These are available from MusiCity.com, J. W. Pepper (www.jwpepper.com), Gamble Music (www.gamblemusic.com), Pender's Music Co. (www.penders.com), Southern Music Co. (www.southernmusic.com), and The Best Box from Tempo Music Office (www.tempomusicoffice.com), among others.

Music folders

Deer River Folio (http://deerriverfolio.com/)

Gamble Music Company leatherette folders (www.gamblemusic.com)

Pajco book and menu covering, available from bookbinders or restaurant supply stores, such as: www.ganebrothers.com or www.foodservicewarehouse.com.

Other supplies

Finally, surround yourself with other quality supplies to help create a quality product: scissors, stapler and stapler remover, pencil sharpener, paper cutter, file folders, and mailing supplies.

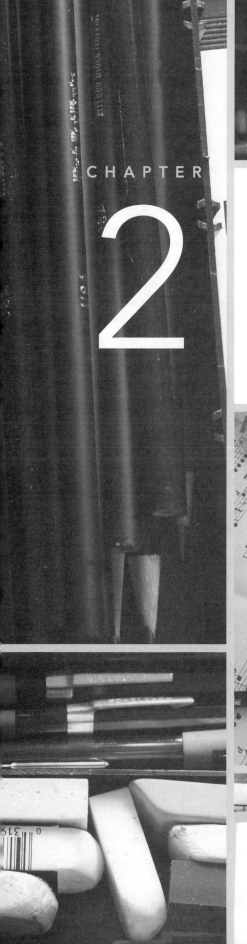

2

ACQUISITIONS

Purchasing Music

When purchasing music, there are several issues that need to be resolved before the order can be placed.

Which edition?

In some cases, there are multiple versions of a single work with different editors, orchestrators, or transcribers. Get a copy of the score your conductor will be using. Your safest bet is to physically have the copy in front of you throughout the typical maze of e-mails and phone conversations with various parties.

Which publisher?

The answer is similar to the suggestion for "which edition" above—get a copy of the score. In some cases, a simple Kalmus will do. In others, an edited Breitkopf & Härtel issue is better. Learn what score your conductor has and match the set to that score. Remember, your role is to prepare the music so rehearsal time is used efficiently on musical issues. If that valuable time is spent with the conductor yelling out rehearsal figures that don't match those in the set, you've failed. If you're just getting started, establish a relationship with a music dealer who can advise you of the different editions and publications available for a single work.

In some cases, your music director may look to you for guidance in which set to purchase. Be mindful of the library's budget in these situations, as you may not be able to afford to spring for the latest and greatest Bärenreiter when your conductor will be just as happy with Kalmus. In some cases though, the library may need to spend a lot of time fixing mistakes in certain editions, so it's a good idea to consult the MOLA errata collection as well. Knowing as much as you can about all alternatives will help you immensely, not to mention make you a smarter librarian.

How many copies?

Make sure you know the string count of your organization. If a choral work, how many choral scores will you need? How many piano/vocal scores will you need for principals, coaches, accompanists, etc.?

How many scores?

Will your conductor want a personal copy of the score? If so, work out payment with the conductor unless your organization covers such expenses. Will you need to order a few smaller, less expensive study scores for your musicians?

Arrival date?

Count backwards from the concert date to ascertain the appropriate need-by date. For example:

Concert Date	September 1	
First rehearsal	August 24	1 week out
Music due to musicians	August 10	3 weeks out
In-library prep: bowings	July 13	7 weeks out
*Principal Bass does bowings**	June 29	9 weeks out
*Principal Cello does bowings**	June 15	11 weeks out
*Principal Viola does bowings**	June 1	13 weeks out
*Principal 2nd does bowings**	May 18	15 weeks out
*Concertmaster does bowings**	April 20	19 weeks out
In library prep: Measure numbers, errata, fix page turns, etc.	March 23	24 weeks out
Music arrives (allow time to fix ordering mistakes, both librarian and vendor errors are possible)	March 2	**27 weeks out (nearly 7 months)**

*These are suggested time frames. Your concertmaster may not need an entire month and the rest of your principals may not require two weeks each to mark their bowings. Also, depending on your personnel, all your principals may only desire to see the concertmaster part. If so, this will eliminate six weeks in the process. However, it's always a good idea to allow time for the worst possible scenario, i.e., your principal second is in Helsinki for several weeks, the principal cellist has bursitis, the principal violist's dog has a penchant for eating music–you get the idea.

According to the overly generous timeline above, you should place your order nearly seven months out. Think of it as childbirth.

Obtain fiscal clearance

Once you've narrowed down which edition and which vendor you will use, get a price quote. Make sure you include shipping in this estimate. Present it to your supervisor or whomever makes the financial decisions in your organization. In some cases, you will need to obtain a purchase order number to present to the vendor who will subsequently issue a bill to your organization. It's always a good idea to have those bills addressed to you in care of your institution so you can monitor their progress and consistency between quotes and bills.

Keeping track

Establish a system for keeping track of all ordering. It can be as simple as a spreadsheet or as complex as a homegrown database in Access or FileMaker. Some prefer using a folder system for paper copies or binders for entire seasons. The important thing is to stay on top of your orders to make sure sets are arriving when they are supposed to and to monitor your budget. Nasty surprises are the bane of any librarian's existence. See the article on "Acquisitions Record Keeping" for further discussion of this topic.

Renting Music

Determine if a work is for rent or purchase

One reliable method of determining the answer to the purchase versus rental dilemma is to consult David Daniels's handy resource, *Orchestral Music: A Handbook*.[1] Alphabetically organized by composer, publisher information is provided immediately following each listing. This can be cross-referenced with the more thorough listing of publisher contact information found in the book's appendix. For band compositions, if you can't find the work for sale through your favorite vendor, it may only be available as a rental. Fortunately, most contemporary band composers have their own website which can be found via a simple Google search.

Obtain a quote

Most publishers prefer that you communicate with them via their online request form which can be readily found on their website. Publishers field many requests in a given day and virtual communication is an excellent way to efficiently streamline the process for both the librarian and the rental agent. Use the publisher's form and submit it as instructed.

When renting a work, you are entering into a small rights agreement with the composer's publisher or the publisher's agent. This agreement allows your ensemble to perform the work in a public venue. Publishers base their rental fee on several parameters that range from the length of the work to the budget of the performing ensemble. The more thoroughly and completely you can supply the needed information, the easier and quicker the process will become.

Possible discounts

- Is your concert free?
- Is the concert an educational effort?
- Will you be performing only a short excerpt of a longer work?

All of these are potential scenarios for a reduced rental rate. A good rule of thumb is to tell the rental agent *everything* about the concert as they can alert you to specific procedures necessary. Remember, you are requesting permission to perform these works from the publisher.

Arrival date

Most rental periods range from six to eight weeks from shipment to performance date. You will not have the luxury of added prep time with a rental that you would with

---

1   David Daniels, *Orchestral Music: A Handbook* (4th ed. Lanham, Md.: Scarecrow Press, 2005). Online version available by subscription at http://www.orchestralmusic.com.

a purchased work unless your organization has deep pockets they would like emptied on extended music rentals (not likely). While six weeks may not seem like a lot of time, there are some remedies that may be employed to alleviate the crush of time. Most rental companies will supply a set of principal strings and score in advance for a small fee. This fee is much less than extending your rental period beyond the base amount. Alert your principals ahead of time that a rental is on its way for a particular program. They, just like you, hate being ambushed at the last minute. One crisis is fine, but when they become epidemic, you lose your credibility. Finally, you can negotiate an extended rental period with the rental agent, but make sure you add that to the quote you are giving to your financial folks. If you can make a strong enough case, they may buy it, literally.

Performance rights organizations

Your organization will need to have a license with the performing rights organization (PRO) that represents the composers' works on your concert. You will need this license in addition to your rental agreement with the publisher. The three main PROs in North America are:

- American Society of Composers, Authors and Publishers (ASCAP)
- Broadcast Music Incorporated (BMI)
- Society of Composers, Authors and Music Publishers of Canada (SOCAN)

These organizations exist to provide compensation to each of the composers they represent. Most large ensembles have blanket licenses that cover all performances for the length of the licensing period, which is typically a year and requires an annual fee. There are also smaller licensing options that can be negotiated on a case-by-case basis. Explore licensing options with each organization to determine the best one for your circumstance.

Get quote approved

Once you have received your quote from the publisher, it will depend on how your organization operates as to how to proceed. Some simply get the quote then generate a purchase requisition that allows the rental order to be placed. Some prefer to review each rental quote on a case-by-case basis. Others gather all the rental quotes in advance of the season to give their administration needed budget information. It's a good rule of thumb to alert someone higher than you of these costs so they can raise the red budget flag. It's also a good idea for the librarian to remain the main contact point between the publisher and the ensemble. Too many cooks in the same kitchen can confuse the myriad of details. This is your job as the librarian to follow this process through to the bitter end.

Place your order

Remember, a quote does not start the machinery in motion to generate the music to be delivered. A quote is not an order. You must then place your order through the publisher's online request form. As mentioned above, it's best for the librarian to place the order directly with the publisher. It's not a good idea for the accountant who doesn't know the difference between Copland and copy machines to be specifying your string count.

The **Music Sales** *Group*

G. Schirmer Rental and Performance Library
445 Bellvale Road
PO Box 572
Chester, NY 10918 USA

phone 845-469-4699
fax 845-469-7544
E-mail rental@schirmer.com

REQUEST FOR RENTAL MATERIALS
Use the TAB key to navigate this form. Click on check-boxes where appropriate.
Print completed form, then mail, fax, or save and attach to an E-mail message.

1 MATERIALS REQUESTED
Composer (and Arranger):

Title:

String parts 9.8.7.6.5 and one score are supplied for all standard orchestral works. Additional scores, parts, and/or permission to copy/augment string parts for practice purposes must be requested at the time of order and are subject to additional charges.
Additional materials requested:

Quantity/language/translation requested for choral/vocal parts:

Are performing materials already on hand? ☐ Yes ☐ No

2 EVENT DETAILS
Organization:

Conductor:

Soloists:

Venues:

Dates of performances and number of performances per day:

Will complete work be performed? ☐ Yes ☐ No
If no, list excerpts and durations of each:

☐ Free admission ☐ Education concert ☐ Reading only
Dramatic staging of opera? ☐ Yes ☐ No
If yes, state house size and ticket prices:

3 BROADCAST AND RECORDING
If broadcast Station call letters:
☐ Web stream
If recording
☐ Archival ☐ Commercial ☐ Podcast ☐ Studio ☐ Live
Record company: Distribution company:

Sale price: Copies to be pressed:

4 PRICE To Request a Quote
Skip steps 5, 6, and 7. Enter name and E-mail address below.
Print form, then mail, fax, or save and attach to an E-mail message.
Name:

E-mail address:

Quote amount (from G. Schirmer):

Revision 20080708

5 CUSTOMER INFORMATION
All new accounts must prepay. G. Schirmer will send you a contract via E-MAIL, FAX, or POSTAL MAIL. Materials will not be shipped without a returned signed contract.
Name:

Attn:

Billing address:

City:

State/province: Zip/postal code:

Country:

County (New York and California only):

E-mail: Fax (required for contract):

6 SHIPPING
We cannot ship to a Post Office Box.
Librarian:

Address:

City:

State/province: Zip/postal code:

Country:

Telephone number (required for shipping):

Shipping via UPS Ground unless you request another method. Additional charges will apply. Other method requested:

Materials are shipped 6 weeks prior to performance. An early charge of $75 per month will be billed for each additional month materials are required.
Delivery date requested:

Materials are due back within 10 days of the last performance. A late charge of $25 per week will be billed for late returns.
7 PERFORMANCE LICENSE FOR CONCERTS
You must be licensed by ASCAP or BMI (or, in Canada, by SOCAN). This does not apply to opera, ballet, liturgical services, or high schools.
ASCAP (1-800-652-7227):

BMI (existing accounts 1-877-264-2137, new accounts 264-2139):

SOCAN (1-800-557-6226):

Example of a publisher's rental form. *Reprinted by Permission of G. Schirmer, Inc.*

Other Sources for Acquiring Music

I f you are a small organization without a large budget to buy or rent music, you have to be creative about acquiring parts to play. The following are a few suggestions of other places to look for performance materials.

Lending libraries and consortiums

Some private and public libraries have collections of performance materials that they will lend to individuals or organizations. They may require a membership fee or charge for each item borrowed. Check the libraries in your area for these types of special collections. Examples include:

The Fleischer Collection at the Free Library of Philadelphia:
http://libwww.library.phila.gov/collections/collectionDetail.cfm?id=14
The New York Public Library Orchestra Collection:
http://www.nypl.org/locations/lpa/orchestra-collection
The San Francisco Public Library orchestral music set collection:
http://sfpl.org/index.php?pg=2000178401
Chatfield Brass Band & Music Lending Library:
http://www.chatfieldband.lib.mn.us/
Paramount Theatre Music Library:
http://www.paramounttheatremusiclibrary.org
Bagaduce Music Lending Library:
http://www.bagaducemusic.org
Arkansas Valley Wind & Percussion Ensemble, Inc.:
http://www.lending-library.com

Educational institutions

State, district, and regional educational associations may have a centralized library for their members to pool resources, including music collections. Ask local music teachers or contact the area headquarters to inquire about these collections.

Area colleges and universities, and occasionally primary and secondary schools, may also be willing to rent, loan, or trade their sets. (There may, however, be school or civic policies that restrict these activities if the music was acquired with dedicated or encumbered funds.) Examples include:

Alberta Band Association (Edmonton, Alberta, Canada):
http://albertabandassociation.com/library.php
Illinois Music Educators Association:
http://www.ilmea.org/MusicLibrary.shtml
Louisiana State University Lucile Blum Lending Library:
http://www.music.lsu.edu/Ensembles/Orchestras/Library.html

Publishers and music dealers

Luck's Music Library and the Edwin F. Kalmus & Co. are in the business of selling music, although both companies also rent some of their publications. Sets available for rent are identified in both companies' print and online catalogs.

The next question is whether to rent this music or buy it outright. If your organization does not want to maintain a library of music, perhaps because of space restrictions, renting may be a better option. If, however, it is a standard repertoire work that your ensemble is likely to play again, purchasing the music may be a better solution. This is particularly true if you will spend a great deal of time on bowing, correcting errata, fixing page turns, and other music preparation issues.

Educational Music Service acquired the Mapleson Music Library collection of opera music, which is available to rent. EMS also has arrangements of pops music, now out of print, that can be rented. Contact them directly for a list of titles. Another service available to orchestras is the EMS collection of bowing masters for standard repertoire works. This is a helpful resource for orchestras that do not have the time or a process in place to create bowings with their own personnel.

Occasionally the rental libraries of large music publishers will offer special rates on some of their works, often in conjunction with anniversaries or seasonal events. Watch for special announcements advertising these deals.

Luck's Music Library: http://www.lucksmusic.com
Edwin F. Kalmus & Co., Inc.: http://www.kalmus-music.com
Educational Music Service: http://www.emsmusic.com

Online and digital resources

The International Music Score Library Project (IMSLP) contains a large collection of digitized music. This is a collaborative effort, collecting scanned images of solo, chamber, and ensemble music in the public domain. The collection is easily searchable, the quality of reproduction is generally good, and publication information for each work is included. Although this is not a comprehensive collection of each composer's works or of every part for a given work, the project is still growing and any gaps will likely be filled over time: http://www.imslp.org.

There are other online collections of sheet music, some free and some for sale. They may contain reproductions of early-published editions or they may include re-engraved parts. Be cautious when choosing from these online sites—examine the parts for quality of reproduction, layout, and attention to detail (errata, accuracy in reproducing dynamics and articulations, etc.). Although not all offer large ensemble works, they may be helpful to locate individual instrumental parts for study, audition preparation, or solo parts for concerti.

FreeHandMusic: http://www.freehandmusic.com
Free Scores.com: http://www.free-scores.com/index_uk.php3
Free Sheet Music.net: http://www.freesheetmusic.net

Musica Viva: http://www.musicaviva.com
Musopen: http://www.musopen.com
Mutopia Project: http://www.mutopiaproject.org
Virtual Sheet Music: http://www.virtualsheetmusic.com

The Orchestra Musician's CD-ROM Library consists of compact discs with scanned PDF images of individual parts from a composer's works (for example, one CD contains trumpet parts for all of Beethoven's symphonies, overtures, and incidental music, and other works). All of the works are in the public domain and are reproductions of standard published editions. It is possible that an orchestra could purchase the Beethoven discs for each instrument so they would then own parts to all nine symphonies. The drawback with this plan is that the librarian has now become a music publisher, responsible for printing and binding all of the parts for their complete ensemble. Only then can they begin the usual library work of bowing, correcting errata, and other part preparation: http://www.orchmusiclibrary.com.

BAND MUSIC
Band Music PDF Library contains complete sets of public domain band music. The bulk of the collection is march-size music, with the occasional work for full band: http://www.bandmusicpdf.org.

The Library of Congress Music for the Nation, American Sheet Music collection, has digitized sheet music from the Library's extensive collection of holdings. Most titles are of piano sheet music, but there are some sets of band parts available for viewing and printing: http://memory.loc.gov/ammem/mussmhtml/mussmhome.html

John Philip Sousa, The March King: http://lcweb2.loc.gov/diglib/ihas/html/sousa/sousa-home.html

African-American Band Music & Recordings, 1883–1923: http://lcweb2.loc.gov/diglib/ihas/html/stocks/stocks-home.html

CHORAL MUSIC
Choral Public Domain Library: http://www2.cpdl.org/wiki

"Free download sites" are listed on the ChoralNet website, sponsored by the American Choral Directors Association: http://www.choralnet.org/list/resource/1939

FOR MORE RESOURCES
Read Martin Jenkins's article in the journal of the Music Library Association: "Digital Media Reviews: Free (Mostly) Scores on the Web," *Notes* 59, no. 2 (December 2002): 403-407. Also visit his web site: Free Printable Music on the Web: A Guide to Internet Resources: http://www.wright.edu/~martin.jenkins/printmusic.html.

Ana Dubnjakovic's article, "Navigating Digital Sheet Music on the Web: Challenges and Opportunities" in *Music Reference Services Quarterly* 12 (2009): 3–15, lists 192 websites that offer digital sheet music online.

Dubnjakovic also suggests the music score indexing website www.free-scores.com as a search engine for locating digital music.

Acquisitions Record Keeping

It is important to keep track of the music you purchase, rent, or borrow, for several reasons:

- Budget planning: A record of your expenses over time will show your annual costs, trends in pricing, and provide documentation for future budget negotiations.
- Work planning: Knowing delivery dates helps to coordinate your library workflow so the parts are ready on schedule.
- Documenting payments and rental returns: If invoices are misplaced or packages are lost in transit, this will record what actions you took and when.

This information can be recorded in a spreadsheet, a database, a columnar list, or even on index cards, although a computer application will allow for easier manipulation of the information to create reports and delivery timetables.

Information to record

The following data fields can be included. They are listed by priority, with the later fields perhaps not vital, but helpful if space allows.

- Title
- Composer
- Performance date
- Item(s) ordered
- Date ordered
- Date due
- Date received
- Date paid
- Date returned (for rental orders)
- Purchase order number (if your organization uses them)
- Cost
- Source (name of publisher and/or music dealer)
- Pending ("yes" or "no")
- Invoice received ("yes" and/or the date received)
- Invoice number (useful when communicating with the publisher or dealer about billing or delivery issues)
- Reference number (some publishers use an internal transaction number, different from the invoice number)
- Budget number or Ensemble (if you control multiple accounts or support more than one group)
- Notes (to record any related information that is pertinent to the order)
- Rental set number (so you can ask for the same set if you perform the work again in the future)

Documents to retain

You should maintain two types of files for all transactions: active and historical. This is where you will hold all the pertinent documents relating to the acquisitions or the concert. The files can be arranged by work, source or dealer, or by performance date. Store them in a file folder system or a three-ring binder for safekeeping and easy reference.

The active files will include all documents on active and forthcoming performances. This should include:

- Rental request forms and/or purchase orders
- Rental contracts
- Set inventories
- Invoices (also include copies of signed or processed invoices to document the date the vendor was paid)
- Any related correspondence or documents

If you fax your orders to the publisher or music dealer, you may also want to print a fax delivery confirmation report, to show when your order was placed and that it was received on the other end.

In the historical files, you can eliminate extraneous documents that have no long-term interest, but you should retain:

- Rental contracts
- Set inventories (specifically those marked to show what parts you received from the rental library)
- Paid invoices
- Any notable related correspondence or documents

The historical files, whether kept in paper and/or electronic form, can be helpful if questions about the work arise years later. These questions could include: source of the material, cost paid (which may help estimate future costs for the same work), and instrumentation. They should be kept in larger document groups arranged by season or fiscal year, ensemble, project, or vendor, depending on which is more efficient for your organization. If you have an archives record retention system in your organization, their requirements may determine how you prepare and submit your historical files.

Receiving Music—Purchases

1. Open the package and remove all the music AND all paperwork (inventories, packing slips, invoices, etc.). Note that some music dealers attach documents to the outside of the package!
2. Mark the date the music was received on the upper right corner of the packing slip as follows: *rec'd 4/5/2011.*
3. Compare the packing slip to the contents.
4. Make a note of any discrepancies between the packing slip and the materials in hand. Notify the music dealer immediately so you are not charged for materials you did not receive.
5. Store the music on the concert shelf, in a safe location, or process it to add to your library collection.
6. You may want to make a temporary folder or storage box to keep all the music together in one place while you are working on it.
7. File the paperwork in your acquisitions notebook.
8. Record the delivery date of the music in your acquisitions log or database.

Receiving Music—Rentals

1. Open the package and remove all the music AND all paperwork (inventories, packing slips, invoices, etc.). Note that some publishers attach documents to the outside of the package!
2. Mark the date the music was received on the upper right corner of the inventory or packing slip as follows: *rec'd 4/5/2011.*
3. Make a photocopy of the publisher's inventory sheet.[2] You will use this to check the music you received and make any notes on the condition of the set.
4. Compare the inventory/packing sheet to the contents and note on your copy of the sheet:

   a) The number of string parts and the number of scores received.
   b) The winds, brass, and percussion inventory. Write the publisher's part number[3] next to the part name.[4] In case a part is missing later, you will know by the number exactly which one it is.

5. Make a note of any discrepancies between the publisher's inventory sheet/ packing slip and the materials in hand. Notify the publisher immediately so you can request any missing parts and so you are not charged for materials you did not receive.
6. Examine the score and the parts to ensure that they match. Check for publication or copyright dates, plate numbers or edition numbers, rehearsal figures, or other discrepancies. Notify the publisher if you have any questions or concerns.
7. Store the music on the concert shelf or in a safe location.
8. You may want to make a temporary folder or storage box to keep all the music together in one place while you are working on it.
9. File the paperwork either with the rental parts, in a separate concert file folder, or in your acquisitions notebook.
10. Record the delivery date of the music in your acquisitions log or database.

---

2   If the publisher has not included an inventory sheet, fill out a blank inventory form (see the Appendix for a sample) to record what was received.

3   Most publishers number their wind sets to speed their inventory process. (See the article on "Numbering Parts.") The publisher's numbering system may differ from your library's system so record the one that appears on their parts.

4   If the publisher has not numbered their parts, assign your own number system (written in pencil on each part) to help with your inventory during the term of your rental.

Acquisitions checklist

After receiving the list of music you need to acquire:

_____ 1. Clarify any uncertain information with your conductor, music director, or soloist, particularly concerning proper form and spelling of titles, composer and/or arranger names, and editions.

_____ 2. Determine if the music is available for purchase or as a rental. See the articles:

- *Purchasing Music*
- *Renting Music*

To stretch your library budget, you may want to consider alternate resources. See the article:

- *Other Sources for Acquiring Music*

_____ 3. Order the music. Contact your music dealer for sale items and contact the music publisher or their representative for rental items.

_____ 4. Document the ordering, expenses, and receipt of the music. See the article:

- *Acquisitions Record Keeping*

_____ 5. Check in the music when you receive it. See the articles:

- *Receiving Music—Purchases*
- *Receiving Music—Rentals*

CHAPTER

3

CATALOGING

Creating Your Library Catalog

I f you need to update your library catalog, migrate it to another format, or create one from scratch, here are some points to consider and a procedure to help with the task.

1. Determine what information to include in your catalog.
The amount of detail you need depends on how it will be used.

The catalog may serve as a surrogate for your collection; that is, you look in the catalog to find what music you have rather than looking at the music itself. This is particularly helpful if your collection is stored in a remote location or if others have access to your catalog only, but not the music.

By recording the right information, your catalog can tell what editions you own, the condition of the music, what bowings are in it, and what rehearsal figures are used. If your conductor or music director uses the catalog for programming ideas, you may also want to include instrumentation, composer dates, subject headings, musical form, the performance history, and perhaps movement titles and timings.

If, however, you only need to know what music you own and where to find it on the shelf, a simpler system may suffice.

2. Determine what kind of catalog format you will use: database, spreadsheet, or catalog cards.
With a database, you can include all of the information above and more. You can create layouts and views to show only the information you need. You can also link other databases so they can all access related information.

A spreadsheet is not as flexible as a database. The information can be searched and sorted, but you cannot easily perform multi-level searches and then create reports from that data.

Card catalogs are the least flexible system. You are limited to the information that will fit on the card itself. Searches require looking at each card and possibly reordering them according to the criteria. At least two cards should be created for each work: one for the composer and one for the title. They can contain the same information, but will be filed differently. Additional cards could be created for other criteria (subject headings or musical forms) to allow other searches.

3. Determine your authority sources and data entry format.
An authority source is used to establish a consistent form and spelling of a name or title. It may be a book, website, or library catalog, but it should be a credible resource. You will use the authority's form and spelling in your catalog to enter data and also to search the catalog so that all incarnations of a work or composer appear together.

Choose a consistent formula for entering titles of works. Don't just enter the title as it is printed on the music, otherwise you may have one entry that reads *Le Sacre du Printemps* and another that reads *The Rite of Spring*. This is particularly important for titles with musical forms, such as Symphony and Concerto. Choose a formula for your catalog and apply it to all titles, so that all concertos appear as Concerto for Flute and are not mistakenly labelled as Flute Concerto, which would be sorted differently in your database.

See the article on "Cataloging Authorities" for more information on this topic.

4. Prepare an inventory sheet.

Fill out an inventory sheet for each set of parts in your library. Most of the information for the catalog database can be taken from this document. Keep the sheet with the parts to show the instrumentation of the work and how many copies of each part you own. A sample inventory sheet can be found in the Appendix.

5. Enter the information into your catalog.

Remember that the two most important considerations when cataloging are accuracy and consistency. If the information you record isn't accurate, you won't be able to locate the item in the library. If the information is not recorded consistently, you won't find all the items that meet your search criteria.

6. Clean the database.

If you have completed a major data entry project, or if you have inherited a library catalog that may have errors or inconsistencies in it, allow some time to proofread the data.

In a database or spreadsheet, select a view option that allows you to see each record in a columnar format (see example). This allows you to examine many records in sequence and more easily compare the data between records with similar information.

No.	Composer	Library Title	Publisher
550	BEETHOVEN, Ludwig van	Symphony no. 2, op. 36, D major	Broude Bros. (New York) [Breitkopf reprint]
551	BEETHOVEN, Ludwig van	Symphony no. 3, op. 55, E-flat major, "Eroica"	Breitkopf & Härtel (Leipzig)
552	BEETHOVEN, Ludwig van	Symphony no. 3, op. 55, E-flat major, "Eroica"	Kalmus (Boca Raton) [Breitkopf reprint]
553	BEETHOVEN, Ludwig van	Symphony no. 3, op. 55, E-flat major, "Eroica"	Breitkopf & Härtel (Wiesbaden)
554	BEETHOVEN, Ludwig van	Symphony no. 3, op. 55, E-flat major, "Eroica"	Bärenreiter

Example: Database columnar display

Sort the data according to the criteria below. Examine each record for correct spelling and formatting. Compare each record against others with similar information so that records with the same information match. For example, if you have three sets of Beethoven's Third Symphony, even if they are from different publishers, the composer name and the title should be exactly the same so that all sets will appear when searching the catalog.

Sort and examine your data as follows:

- Composer
- Title

- Composer, then by title (sort on both fields simultaneously)
- Arranger / Editor
- Publisher
- Accession number (to see if you have any unused or duplicate numbers)

Watch for data records that are out of order. Be aware that the smallest detail can affect how records sort and ultimately how they are searched. Check for:

- Placement of punctuation marks (periods, commas, quotation marks)
- Inverted letters (teh instead of the) which can be easily overlooked
- Two or more unintentional blank spaces between words or characters

Once the data is proofread, compare any new acquisitions with existing entries to be sure you are consistent in your typing and your choice of formatting.

Cleaning your data can be tedious and time-consuming work. Allow enough uninterrupted time to complete the project, or break it into smaller chunks and stay focused. It is a worthwhile endeavor.

Cataloging Authorities

The two most important considerations when cataloging are accuracy and consistency. If the information you record isn't accurate, you won't be able to locate the appropriate item in the library catalog. If the information is not recorded consistently, you won't find all of the items that meet your search criteria. It is essential that you enter details about the piece properly so that you can locate the music quickly and efficiently when it is needed.

For example, Piotr Ilyich Tchaikovsky's name appears in different spellings depending on the music publisher or reference book you consult:

Tchaikowsky
Tschaikowsky
Chaikovski
Chaikovsky

Music titles may also appear in different forms and spellings:

Klavierkonzert Nr. 5, Es-Dur, op. 73
Konzert für Klavier und Orchester Nr. 5, Es-Dur, op. 73
Concerto for Piano in Eb major, op. 73
Piano Concerto no. 5 in E-flat major, op. 73, "Emperor"

For composer names, choose a book, catalog, or other resource to be an "authority" source that you can consult to determine the spelling of all names entered in the catalog. For example, if you are cataloging Shostakovich's Fifth Symphony, always use the spelling of Shostakovich that you find in your authority source. Also make sure that all works by Shostakovich are spelled the same way in your library catalog. Then be sure to use this same spelling when you search for works by Shostakovich so that all of your holdings appear together in your database or card catalog.

For composition titles, choose an authority source that applies a consistent format to all titles. Be aware that there are two types of titles:

1. The "form title" or "generic title" that includes a musical form, such as Symphony, Concerto, Divertimento, etc.
2. The "descriptive" or "distinctive" title, such as "The Planets" or "Don Juan."

Form title entries

Form titles must include as many pertinent details as possible to help identify the exact work you are describing. There are many works called "Symphony No. 5," but by including the key and opus number, you can distinguish Beethoven's work from Tchaikovsky's work.

Elements to include when constructing a form title:

Musical form (symphony, concerto, etc.)
Medium of performance (piano, cello, band, etc.—if necessary)

Serial number (no. 5)
Opus number or thematic index number (op. 101, K. 364)
Key (A major, E-flat minor)
Descriptive title ("Emperor", "Pathétique")

Include as many elements as apply to the work, omitting those that do not apply. Using the format above will yield the following titles:

Symphony no. 6, op. 74, B minor, "Pathétique"
Concerto for Piano, no. 5, op. 73, E-flat major, "Emperor"
Rondo for Violin and String Orchestra, D. 438, A major

In the examples above, the medium of performance is not included for the Symphony because it is implied that a symphony is most commonly written for the orchestra. If the symphony was for band or another ensemble, that information should be included, such as "Symphony for Band, no. 6." Similarly, for the Rondo, "String Orchestra" is included because it specifies a medium other than the full orchestra.

Pay attention to the use and location of spaces and punctuation. This will affect how the catalog cards are filed and also how the computer will search and sort the words.

Other cataloging rules

Excerpts from a larger work. If a selection is taken from a larger composition, such as a movement from a suite or an aria from an opera, list the larger work first, then the excerpt, so that all parts of the larger work appear together in the catalog. Separate the larger work from the excerpt with a colon:

Candide: Make Our Garden Grow
Candide: Overture
Concerto for Piano, no. 5, op. 73, E-flat major, "Emperor": 2. Adagio un poco mosso
Cosi fan tutte, K. 588: Overture
Cosi fan tutte, K. 588: Soave sia il vento

Initial articles. Articles that appear at the beginning of a title should be inverted so that the first significant word of the title appears at the beginning of the card or data field. Move the article to the end of the title, preceded by a comma and a blank space. The remainder of the title elements (medium, opus, key, etc.) will follow, as appropriate:

Stars and Stripes Forever, The
Magic Flute, The, K. 610: Overture
Francs-juges, Les, op. 3: Overture
Wand of Youth, The: Suite no. 1, op. 1a

Common articles include:

a, an (English, Hungarian, Irish, Scots)
das, dem, den der, des, die (Danish, German, Norwegian, Swedish)
ein, eine, einem, einen, einer, eines (German)
l', la, le, les, lo, los (French, Italian, Spanish)
the (English)
un, una, une (French, Italian, Romanian, Spanish)

Language of titles. If you prefer titles to be in your native language because it is more familiar to your users, then simply ensure that all works are entered consistently. For example, if you prefer English language titles in your catalog, you would enter some works as follows:

The Magic Flute (not Die Zauberflöte)
The Firebird (not L'Oiseau de feu or Zhar-ptitsa)
The Barber of Seville (not Il Barbiere di Siviglia)

However, some works may be more familiar in the original, rather than the translated title:

Symphonie Fantastique (not Fantastic Symphony)
Ein Heldenleben (not A Hero's Life)
Die Fledermaus (not The Bat)

If you have a field for "alternate title" in your database, these secondary or translated titles may be entered there so that they may also be searched.

Resources for Cataloging

S ome of the same resources used for locating music for acquisition can also be used for cataloging. This is especially true for new works or unfamiliar composers. In these cases, it may be helpful to add a cataloging note to your database or card catalog that indicates the source where the information was found. This can be helpful if the data is questioned, needs updating, or when cataloging other works by the same composer.

Print resources

The standard books on orchestra repertoire will tell a work's title, composer, instrumentation, and publisher. They may not include additional bibliographic information (publication date, edition number), but they will provide the basic details to enter into the catalog.

COMPOSER NAMES AND WORK LISTS

Sadie, Stanley, editor. John Tyrrell, executive editor. *The New Grove Dictionary of Music and Musicians*. 2nd ed. New York: Grove's Dictionaries, 2001. 29 volumes. Online edition edited by Deane Root. http://www.oxfordmusiconline.com.

Baker, Theodore. *Baker's Biographical Dictionary of Musicians*. Nicolas Slonimsky, editor emeritus. Laura Kuhn, Baker's series advisory editor. 9th ed. New York: Schirmer Books, 2001. 6 volumes.

Gilder, Eric. *The Dictionary of Composers and Their Music: A Listener's Companion*. New York: Wings Books, 1985.

ORCHESTRA

Daniels, David. *Orchestral Music: A Handbook*. 4th ed. Lanham, Md.: Scarecrow Press, 2005. Available online by subscription at http://www.orchestralmusic.com.

Deutsches Musikarchiv der Deutschen Nationalbibliothek, editors. *Bonner Katalog: Verzeichnis reversgebundener musikalischer Aufführungsmateriale* [The Bonn Catalog: Index of Rental Materials for Musical Performances]. 4th ed. in print. Munich: K.G. Saur-Verlag, 2000. 13th ed. on CD-ROM. Munich: K. G. Saur, 2010.

Farish, Margaret K. *Orchestral Music in Print*. Philadelphia, Pa.: Musicdata, 1979. Supplements 1983, 1994, 1999. Available online by subscription at http://www.emusicinprint.com.

Koshgarin, Richard. *American Orchestral Music: A Performance Catalog*. Metuchen, N.J.: Scarecrow Press, 1992.

Saltonstall, Cecilia D., and Henry Saltonstall. *A New Catalog of Music for Small Orchestra*. Clifton, N.J.: European American Music, 1978.

BAND

Gillaspie, Jon A., Marshall Stoneham, and David Lindsey Clark. *The Wind Ensemble Catalog*. Music Reference Collection Series, 63. Westport, Conn.: Greenwood Press, 1998.

Rehrig, William H. *The Heritage Encyclopedia of Band Music*. Paul E. Bierley, editor. Westerville, Ohio: Integrity Press, 1991. 2 volumes. Supplement (Volume 3), 1997. An updated version is available on CD-ROM from Walking Frog Records (Oskaloosa, Iowa), 2005.

Renshaw, Jeffrey H. *The American Wind Symphony Commissioning Project: A Descriptive Catalog of Published Editions, 1957-1991*. New York: Greenwood Press, 1991.

Wallace, David, and Eugene Corporon. *Wind Ensemble/Band Repertoire*. Greeley: University of Northern Colorado, School of Music, 1984.

Whitwell, David. *The History and Literature of the Wind Band and Wind Ensemble*. Northridge, Calif.: Winds (Box 513, Northridge, CA 91328), 1982–1991. 12 volumes.

CHORAL MUSIC

DeVenney, David P. *Nineteenth-Century American Choral Music*. Berkeley, Calif.: Fallen Leaf Press, 1987.
Also by the same author and publisher:
Early American Choral Music: An Annotated Guide. (1988).
American Masses and Requiems: A Descriptive Guide. (1990).
American Choral Music Since 1920: An Annotated Guide. (1993).

Green, Jonathan. *A Conductor's Guide to Choral-Orchestral Works*. Metuchen, N.J.: Scarecrow Press, 1994.
Also by the same author and publisher:
A Conductor's Guide to Choral-Orchestral Works, Twentieth Century, Part II. (1998).
A Conductor's Guide to the Choral-Orchestral Works of J. S. Bach. (2000).
A Conductor's Guide to Choral-Orchestral Works, Classical Period. Volume 1: Haydn and Mozart. (2002).
A Conductor's Guide to Nineteenth-Century Choral-Orchestral Works. (2008).

Rosewall, Michael. *Directory of Choral-Orchestral Music*. New York, London: Routledge, 2007.

OPERA

Eaton, Quaintance. *Opera Production: A Handbook*. Volume One: Minneapolis: University of Minnesota Press, 1961. Reprint, New York: Da Capo, 1974. Volume Two: Minneapolis: University of Minnesota Press, 1974.

Holden, Amanda, editor. *The New Penguin Opera Guide*. London, New York: Penguin Books, 2001.

Kornick, Rebecca Hodell. *Recent American Opera: A Production Guide*. New York: Columbia University Press, 1991.

Martin, Nicholas Ivor. *The Da Capo Opera Manual*. New York: Da Capo Press, 1997.

Summers, W. Franklin. *Operas in One Act: A Production Guide*. Lanham, Md.: Scarecrow Press, 1997.

POPULAR MUSIC, JAZZ, MUSICAL THEATER, AND FILM

Bloom, Ken. *American Song: The Complete Companion to Tin Pan Alley Song*. New York: Schirmer Books, 2001. 2 volumes.

———. *American Song: The Complete Film and Musical Companion*. New York: Facts on File, 1995. 3 volumes.

———. *American Song: The Complete Musical Theater Companion*. New York: Facts on File, 1985. 2 volumes.

DeVenney, David P. *The New Broadway Song Companion: An Annotated Guide to Musical Theater Literature by Voice Type and Song Style*. Lanham, Md.: Scarecrow Press, 2009.

Kernfeld, Barry. *The New Grove Dictionary of Jazz*. 2nd ed. New York: Grove's Dictionaries, 2002. 3 volumes. Online edition at http://www.oxfordmusiconline.com.

Larkin, Colin. *The Encyclopedia of Popular Music*. 4th ed. Oxford: Oxford University Press, 2006. 8 volumes. Online edition at http://www.oxfordmusiconline.com.

Lissauer, Robert. *Lissauer's Encyclopedia of Popular Music in America. 1888 to the Present*. New York: Facts on File, 1996. 3 volumes.

Manning, Lucy. *Orchestral "Pops" Music: A Handbook*. Lanham, Md.: Scarecrow Press, 2009.

OTHER COMPOSER AND TITLE RESOURCES

Berkowitz, Freda Pastor. *Popular Titles and Subtitles of Musical Compositions*. 2nd ed. Metuchen, N.J.: Scarecrow Press, 1975.

Chwiałkowski, Jerzy. *The Da Capo Catalog of Classical Music Compositions*. New York: Da Capo Press, 1996.

Hodgson, Julian. *Music Titles in Translation: A Checklist of Musical Compositions*. London: Clive Bingley; Hamden, Conn.: Linnet, 1976.

Pallay, Steven G. *Cross Index Title Guide to Classical Music*. Westport, Conn.: Greenwood Press, 1987.

———. *Cross Index Title Guide to Opera and Operetta*. Westport, Conn.: Greenwood Press, 1989.

Online resources

Because the process of cataloging can sometimes be a time-consuming task, it can be helpful to gather information from other sources and enter that in your catalog, rather than create it from scratch. Broadly speaking, this is known as "copy cataloging" and is common in the library field. The goal is to find another library or bibliographic source that has cataloged the same item you have, then copy that information into your library catalog or database. Ideally, this will provide you with accurate spellings, title formats, and bibliographic information which was created and approved by another cataloger.

The hard part is to find a source that includes information for large ensemble works. College and university online library catalogs may include the scores but not always the matching sets of parts for orchestral or band works.

The Aria Database.
   http://www.aria-database.com
Chatfield Brass Band & Music Lending Library.
   http://www.chatfieldband.lib.mn.us
Edwin A. Fleisher Collection of Orchestral Music, Free Library of Philadelphia.
   http://libwww.library.phila.gov/collections/collectionDetail.cfm?id=14
Encore! International Association of Music Libraries, Archives and Documentation Centres, United Kingdom and Ireland Branch. (The online union catalog of sets of performance music in United Kingdom libraries.)
   http://www.peri.nildram.co.uk/encore.htm
Hong Kong Leisure and Cultural Services Department Music Office Library Catalog.
   http://mo.lcsd.gov.hk
Indiana University Libraries, Performing Ensembles Division. (Sign in with "Guest Access"; Choose "location: Cook Music Library - Performing Ensembles Div: Ask PED Staff")
   http://www.iucat.iu.edu
Interlochen Center for the Arts (Choose "Item Type" = Band Parts, Choir Parts, Jazz Band Parts, or Orchestra Parts)
   http://library.interlochen.org/rooms/portal/page/21315_Search_the_Catalog
International Music Score Library Project (IMSLP) and the Petrucci Music Library.
   http://imslp.org/wiki/
Musica International, the Virtual Choral Library.
   http://www.musicanet.org/en/index.php
Wind Repertory Project.
   http://windrep.org
Major publisher's websites:
   http://www.boosey.com
   http://www.eamdllc.com
   http://www.edition-peters.com/home.php
   http://www.presser.com
   http://www.schirmer.com

Score Identification

The following examples illustrate the different types of scores that are typically seen in performance libraries.

The **full score** shows all the parts of the ensemble, usually printed in a format large enough to be used by a conductor. They can range in size from 8½ × 11 inches to 11 × 17 inches and larger.

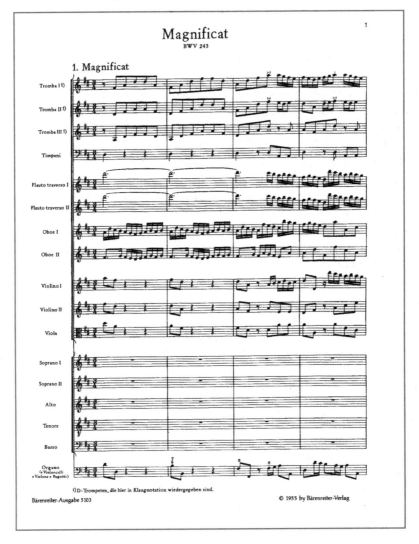

Reproduced by permission of Bärenreiter Verlag.

This example measured 9 × 11⅞ inches or about 28 cm tall.[1]

---

1 Libraries that catalog their materials according to the Anglo-American Cataloguing Rules (AACR) measure scores in centimeters and record only the height in the bibliographic record.

The first page usually shows all of the instruments that play in the work, while subsequent pages may show only those instruments playing at that point in the music. The instruments are arranged in score order from top to bottom, grouped by families (woodwinds, brass, percussion, strings) and organized by pitch, highest to lowest, within that family.

A **miniature score** (also known as a study score or pocket score) looks the same as a full score, and is often reproduced from the same plates, but is reduced in size. They can range from 5¼ × 7¼ inches to 6½ × 8⅞ inches and anywhere in between. They are intended to be used for study purposes and not as a conducting score.

A **condensed score** (also called a compressed or short score) shows the principal voices and harmonies of the work reduced to two or more staves, often with cues to indicate instrumental entrances or solos. This kind of score is often seen with older band sets or educational publications and can be used as a conducting score.

Music for use by a chorus is printed either with or without piano accompaniment. They are usually octavo size, measuring approximately $7 \times 10\frac{1}{2}$ inches.

A **vocal score** shows all of the voice parts with the accompaniment reduced to a two stave part for performance by a keyboard player. It is intended to be used for rehearsing the chorus and as a practice or study score for the vocalists. It may also be used for a performance when only a piano accompaniment is used.

Reproduced by permission of Bärenreiter Verlag.

A **chorus score** shows only the chorus parts with the accompaniment, if included, arranged for a keyboard instrument. These scores generally do not include any solo vocal parts, which would appear in a vocal score.

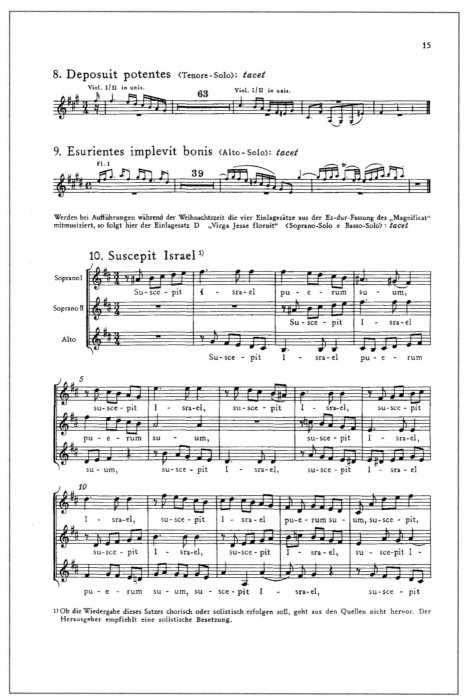

Reproduced by permission of Bärenreiter Verlag.

A **piano-vocal score** shows the voice part above a piano accompaniment. It is used for popular music song sheets or songs accompanied by piano, but usually not for piano reductions of larger ensemble works.

A **piano score** is a reduction of music for a larger ensemble condensed to a grand staff to be performed by a pianist. This is often used for a piano accompaniment to an instrumental concerto or an operatic aria.

Reproduced by permission of Bärenreiter Verlag.

A **close score** shows all of the vocal parts on a minimum number of staves, usually two. This format is often used with hymns.

An **instrumental part** shows only the music for that instrument or voice within the larger ensemble.

Reproduced by permission of Bärenreiter Verlag.

Shelf Arrangement and Filing Systems

I t is vital to arrange your music on the shelf or in the drawer so that you can find it when you need it. Depending on the size and diversity of your collection, this can be a simple or a multi-faceted system, with as many layers of complexity as necessary.

Shelf arrangement

When deciding how to arrange and identify the music, examine the collection and answer the following questions:

1. What ensembles are supported with the collection?

   a) Band
   b) Orchestra
   c) Chorus
   d) Opera
   e) Jazz
   f) Chamber

2. Within those ensembles, are there any related or smaller ensemble holdings that should be kept separate from the other materials?

   a) Marching band, pep band, brass band
   b) String orchestra, chamber orchestra, pops orchestra, educational materials
   c) Women's or men's chorus, children's chorus
   d) Big band, jazz combo, fake books
   e) Historical, rare, or fragile materials

3. Within the ensembles, do you want to arrange the music according to musical form or function?

   a) Symphonies, overtures, concertos and solos, marches
   b) Holiday music, patriotic music

This arrangement is helpful if your conductor likes to browse the collection and examine the music for programming ideas.

4. Are there materials of differing sizes that should be shelved separately, in order to make efficient use of the space available?

   a) March-size parts (5×7 inches) vs. Concert-size parts ($8\frac{1}{2} \times 11$ inches and larger)
   b) Oversize scores or parts (11×15 inches and larger)

5. Do you want to keep these materials separate or shelve them all together?

This decision will be determined in part by the amount of storage space you have available and the number of people who will have access to the collection.

Storage by size or type

Typically, most libraries group the music together by ensemble type, so that like items are shelved together.

Oversize scores and parts are usually stored in a separate location so that the shelving units for the majority of the collection can be set at the same height for a more efficient use of space.

Similarly, sets of small parts, such as march-size music, may be shelved separately or possibly housed in a full-sized folder so that the small parts are not lost or misplaced within the larger envelopes.

Rare, historical, or fragile sets may be shelved in a different location from the working collection, so the music does not receive unnecessary handling or use.

Filing systems

After the decision of how to organize the materials, next determine how to label them so they can be found on the shelf.

The simplest arrangement is by accession number. Assign each set of parts a sequential number from 1 until you reach the end of the collection. Each new set will receive the next number in sequence and will be shelved at the end of the collection. This system works well with large or growing collections because it allows for unlimited expansion and provides a specific location for each item. Each work must, however, be recorded using a computer database or card catalog system and it is this system that will be used to sort and search the collection and to tell the number and location of the work. If the information is recorded incorrectly or a folder is mislabeled, the music can disappear inside the collection.

Another possibility is arrangement alphabetically by the composer's last name, then sub-arranged by the title of the work. This lends itself more easily to browsing, although it does not preclude the need for a card or computer catalog. It also requires a consistent approach to labeling and sorting the music, so that, for example, all concertos are shelved under "Concerto for..." and not also "Piano Concerto" or "Konzert." (See the article on "Cataloging Authorities" for more information on this concept.) You must also leave space on the shelves to accommodate new works added to the collection or be prepared to shift folders in order to fit a new copy of the Beethoven Fifth Symphony in its appropriate alphabetical position.

These were the two most common filing systems in use by members of the Major Orchestra Librarians' Association, as determined by a survey. There are, however, many other possible systems, limited only by the needs of the library or the imagination of the librarian. Some examples include:

- Using a prefix letter or character followed by an accession number: B for band music, O for orchestra music, PE for percussion ensemble, etc., plus a sequential accession number to identify the specific title: B-12 or O-155. This allows music to be grouped by ensemble and easily identified as part of that classification.
- Similar to the example above, use a prefix letter (or letters) for the genre or form of a work, such as P for pops or C for concerto.
- Assign a range of numbers to a given genre, so that catalog numbers 1 to 100 are brass ensemble, numbers 101 to 200 are woodwind ensemble, etc. A drawback to this system is that it restricts the growth of any given section to the numbers allotted.
- Assign a prefix letter based on the composer's last name, followed by an accession number, so that C-100 could be Copland's Fanfare for the Common Man, for example. However, if you want all the works of a given composer to be shelved together, you will have to assign a range of numbers to each composer to accommodate future growth.

Any system you choose should be easy to apply, easy to interpret by librarians and library users, and allow for flexibility and growth.

Subject Access to the Performance Library Catalog

Identifying works of music that fit a specific theme or topic can easily turn into a trivia quiz for the library staff, forcing everyone to search their memories for appropriate works or examine each item in the library for a suitable connection. Even then, many pieces could be overlooked because a connection wasn't obvious by simply reading the title on the music.

While there are a few helpful reference books that classify music by subject, a better solution may be to index your music collection by assigning words and phrases that describe what the music is about. This will provide another level of access to your library collection and help identify music that could be played on a theme concert or to honor a specific person or group. By typing these terms into a searchable field of your library database or creating a set of index cards for each subject heading, you will have fast access to this information.

For example, to program a concert with a "winter" theme you could search the subject field in your database to find music about that season. A well-indexed collection will identify works with an explicit as well as an implicit affiliation, so that you find all music with "winter" in the title, as well as those pieces *about* winter or winter-related activities. Your search might identify movements from *The Seasons* by Vivaldi, Glazunov, or Haydn, as well as "The Skaters" waltz, the "Troika" from *Lieutenant Kije*, or Leroy Anderson's "Sleigh Ride."

When identifying subject terms for your music collection, the most important step is to document which terms are used. Keep a list of the subjects, arranged either alphabetically or grouped by topic (Sport: baseball, bowling, hockey, etc.; Holiday: Christmas, Independence Day, Thanksgiving, etc.). This will ensure that the same word or phrase is used consistently. Consult your list of subject terms when cataloging or searching to be sure you are using the approved term.

You will also need to make decisions on how to apply your subject terms. For example, if a work is suitable for a graduation ceremony, do you use "commencement" or "graduation" or "processional?" Do you combine terms, such as "processional march?" Select a term that is familiar enough to be remembered and also broad enough to apply to the "Pomp and Circumstance" marches, "Academic Festival Overture," or other music that is suitable for the occasion.

Words that describe the musical form of a work can also be included in the subject field, so that all overtures, suites, or arias can be located with a single search term. You can combine search terms here as well to identify a Broadway medley or an opera march.

As your list of terms becomes more detailed, a thesaurus format can be used to indicate which are the preferred index terms and also show cross-references from other terms with USE and USE FOR entries:

Commencement	USE Graduation	
Graduation	USE FOR	Commencement
		Convocation

The thesaurus format can also indicate hierarchical relationships between terms:

Broader Term (BT)

	Heart	**BT**	Anatomy

Narrower Term (NT)

	Dance	**NT**	Fox Trot
			Polka
			Waltz

Related Term (RT)

	Garden	**RT**	Flower

The subject terms should also be flexible enough to allow detailed words or phrases, as needed. For example, geographic names could be entered with their broader classification, such as "City: Seattle" and "State: Washington," or "City: Paris" and "Country: France." In addition to identifying the specific location, this will allow for broader searches using the terms "City," "State," or "Country," to show all works that fit those categories. Most databases and search engines allow searches using phrases set off in quotation marks to find exact matches of your terms. In this way a search written as "brass band" will not also find works for brass ensemble or concert band.

Remember that an index is only as helpful as the amount of information it contains. For each work, include as many terms as possible to ensure the widest coverage of subjects. For example, the song "Oklahoma!" could be described with several terms: State: Oklahoma; Country: U.S.; Musical: Broadway; Musical: Movie; State Song.

Reference Books

There are only a few books that classify music by subject. Some will be invaluable when searching for appropriate works while others may be more helpful by suggesting subject terms that can be used to classify your own library collection.

For "classical" music, a handy reference is Jennifer Goodenberger's *Subject Guide to Classical Instrumental Music* (Metuchen, N.J.: Scarecrow Press, 1989; 1st paperback ed.: Lanham, Md.: Scarecrow Press, 2001). Goodenberger focuses on instrumental art music from the 1600s through the twentieth century, grouping the works into 208 subjects with cross-references to related topics. Written primarily for radio and television programmers, it is not a comprehensive survey, but it does include many standard works.

Klaus Schneider has written two books that classify and categorize instrumental music. Both are in German, but can be easily used for reference without a reading comprehension of the language. The *Lexikon Programmusik* [Encyclopedia of Program Music] (Kassel: Bärenreiter, 1999–2000. 2 volumes) classifies 6,300 instrumental works from the sixteenth to the twentieth century into 147 thematic categories in volume 1. Volume 2 lists works about individuals, real and invented (historical, literary, and mythological), arranged alphabetically by name. A composer index to the works included appears in the back of each volume.

Schneider's *Lexikon "Musik über Musik": Variationen—Transkriptionen—Hommagen—Stilimitationen—B-A-C-H* [Encyclopedia of Music about Music: Variations—Transcriptions—Tributes—Style Imitation—(compositions using) B-A-C-H] (Kassel: Bärenreiter, 2004) lists instrumental music written about, influenced by, or in honor of other music and musicians. The largest category (music about individual composers and their works, pp. 11–321) is arranged by the subject of the music, so that both Liadov's and Rimsky-Korsakov's "Variations on a Theme of Glinka" appear under the entry for Glinka. The other topical lists are helpful and interesting to browse, such as "music that introduces the orchestra and its instruments" (pp. 343–376). Each entry includes the medium of performance (orchestra, piano, string quartet), publisher, and publication date.

Alexander Reischert's *Kompendium der musikalischen Sujets: ein Werkkatalog* [Compendium of Musical Subjects: A Catalog of Works] (Kassel: Bärenreiter, 2001. 2 volumes) lists works based on real individuals and fictional characters from history, literature, mythology, and religion. Volume 2 indexes the first volume by subject and also by name (composer, librettist, author, choreographer, etc.). Reischert intends to keep his books updated with additions and corrections listed on his website (www.musiksujets.de) under the heading "Neues und Ergänzendes zu einzelnen Sujets" [New and supplementary individual subjects].

A helpful general music resource is *The Great Song Thesaurus* by Roger Lax and Frederick Smith (2nd ed. New York: Oxford University Press, 1989). In addition to categorized lists of award-winning songs and theme and trademark songs, the "Thesaurus of Song Titles by Subject, Key Word, and Category" (pp. 621–719) classifies about 11,000 American and British popular songs from the thirteenth century through the 1980s. The 2,300 subject headings are arranged alphabetically with cross-references to other topics.

An index of lesser known popular songs is *The Stecheson Classified Song Directory* by Anthony and Anne Stecheson (Hollywood, Calif.: The Music Industry Press, 1961). While the song titles themselves may not be familiar, the "Song Category Table of Contents" (pp. vi–ix) lists almost 400 categories that can be used as possible subject terms in your own library index. Note that the 1978 Supplement to this directory is not helpful for this purpose.

For subject classification of popular song titles, the most comprehensive reference is *The Green Book of Songs by Subject* by Jeff Green (Nashville, Tenn.: Professional Desk References, 5th ed. 2002. Available by subscription at http://greenbookofsongs.com/default.asp). Compiled for use by radio stations, it categorizes 35,000 recorded songs of the twentieth century. While not helpful for classical music, it uses a wide variety of unique subject headings (1,800 themes), including twenty-five romance-related categories ranging from "falling in love" to "forbidden love" to "get lost!"

Finally, for a traditional library cataloger's approach, *Music Subject Headings: Compiled from Library of Congress Subject Headings*, compiled by Harriette Hemmasi (Lake Crystal, Minn.: Soldier Creek Press, 1998) extracts appropriate music-related subjects from the five volumes of Library of Congress subject headings. The book includes musical form headings (marches, symphonies, zarzuelas) and descriptive headings (campaign songs, children's songs, chance music) arranged in a thesaurus format with extensive cross-references. Hemmasi filters a great deal of information down to a single volume and includes headings to classify works by subject as well as musical form.

Online Resources

Several online resources and thesauri are available which list terms and subject headings in specialized fields of study. They are most helpful when compiling your own subject lists by showing terms commonly used in other disciplines.

The American Society of Indexers provides several links to online thesauri through their website (http://www.asindexing.org/i4a/pages/index.cfm?pageid=3625), such as The Art & Architecture Thesaurus, Astronomy Thesaurus, The Getty Thesaurus of Geographic Names, and many others. Their list of "Reference Sources on the Internet" (http://www.asindexing.org/site/refbooks.shtml) has links to other informational sites which include suitable subject terms but are not arranged as thesauri, such as the Hacker's Jargon Dictionary and the Biographical Dictionary.

The American Folklore Society sponsors an Ethnographic Thesaurus (http://www.afsnet.org/?page=AFSET) which has a searchable feature to suggest terms in folklore, ethnomusicology, cultural anthropology, and related fields, and includes direct access to word lists by category (music, dance, art, etc.).

Yale University's music library cataloging guide (http://www.library.yale.edu/cataloging/music/musicat.htm) has many files and links to cataloging aids, including a page listing types of compositions used in music uniform titles. This link shows preferred terms for musical forms: http://www.library.yale.edu/cataloging/music/types.htm.

For more information about developing your own thesaurus, Tim Craven at the University of Western Ontario has an online tutorial that teaches thesaurus terminology and construction: http://publish.uwo.ca/~craven/677/thesaur/main00.htm.

Cataloging checklist

It is essential to be able to identify, describe, and locate the music in your collection. Follow these steps when cataloging your music.

_____ 1. If your library does not have a card catalog or database, create one. Your existing catalog may also need updating, expansion, or cleaning. See the article:

- *Creating Your Library Catalog*

_____ 2. Standardize the way you enter titles and composer names in your catalog to make it easier to find your music. See the article:

- *Cataloging Authorities*

_____ 3. Identify information sources that will assist you when cataloging. See the article:

- *Resources for Cataloging*

_____ 4. When cataloging, it is important to be able to identify and describe the different forms of scores and parts that you own. See the article:

- *Score Identification*

_____ 5. Determine how to arrange the music on your library shelves and how to identify it with a filing system. See the article:

- *Shelf Arrangement and Filing Systems*

Reproducible forms to assist with cataloging are available in the Appendix.

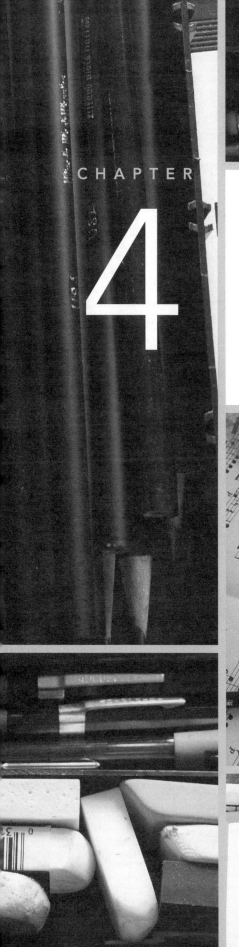

4

PROCESSING

Score Order

"S core order" refers to the arrangement of the instruments and/or voices as they appear reading from the top to the bottom of the page in a conductor's full score.

This order usually reflects the pitch range of the instruments within their families:

- woodwinds
- brass
- percussion
- strings

Unfortunately, the order of instruments is not standardized between composers or publishers and the format of any given score may vary from one composition to another. Therefore, you should adopt a score order for your library that will be used when sorting, collecting, and taking inventory of the music. By establishing and applying this arrangement to all parts, music folders, and written documentation in the library, the instruments will always appear in a consistent and predictable order and missing items will be easily identified.

Once the parts in a set are arranged in score order, they can be numbered (1, 2, 3…) so they are easier to collate in the future.

Here are typical score order arrangements for orchestra, band, and jazz ensemble:

Orchestra

Flute 1
Flute 2
Piccolo
Alto Flute
Oboe 1
Oboe 2
English Horn
Clarinet 1
Clarinet 2
E-flat Clarinet
Bass Clarinet
Bassoon 1
Bassoon 2
Contrabassoon
Soprano Saxophone°
Alto Saxophone
Tenor Saxophone
Baritone Saxophone

°Some libraries put saxophones after clarinets because of stage seating and doubling situations.

Horn 1
Horn 2
Horn 3
Horn 4°

°Wagner Tubas follow Horns, first B-flat tenor, then F bass instruments.

Trumpet 1
Trumpet 2
Trumpet 3°

°Cornets follow Trumpets.

Trombone 1
Trombone 2
Trombone 3 (or Bass Trombone)°

°Tenor Tuba (Euphonium) follows Trombones.

Tuba
Timpani
Percussion°

°Arranged in a consistent fashion, such as Snare Drum, Bass Drum/Cymbals,
Accessory Instruments, Mallet Instruments.

Harp
Piano°

°Followed by other keyboard instruments, such as Celesta, Organ, Accordion,
Synthesizer, etc.

Other instruments: Electric Bass, Guitar, Banjo, Electronic Tape, etc.
1st Violin
2nd Violin
Viola
Cello
Double Bass

Band and Wind Ensemble

Flute 1
Flute 2
Piccolo (C and D-flat)
Alto Flute
Oboe 1
Oboe 2
English Horn
E-flat Clarinet
B-flat Clarinet 1
B-flat Clarinet 2

B-flat Clarinet 3
Alto Clarinet
Bass Clarinet
Contrabass Clarinet (E-flat and B-flat)
Bassoon 1
Bassoon 2
Contrabassoon
Soprano Saxophone°
1st Alto Saxophone
2nd Alto Saxophone
Tenor Saxophone
Baritone Saxophone
Bass Saxophone

°Some libraries put saxophones after clarinets because of stage seating and doubling situations.

Cornet 1
Cornet 2
Cornet 3
Trumpets 1
Trumpet 2°

°Some libraries and music publishers list Horns before Cornets and Trumpets. This has the advantage of maintaining consistency between orchestra and band inventories within the same library.

Horn 1
Horn 2
Horn 3
Horn 4°

°Parts for F and E-flat horns (found in many old band sets and marches) may be transpositions of the same part or different parts requiring separate players.

Trombone 1
Trombone 2
Trombone 3 (or Bass Trombone)
Euphonium/Baritone Treble Clef°
Euphonium/Baritone Bass Clef°

°These may be transpositions of the same part or different parts requiring separate players.

Tuba (marked as Basses in some sets)
Double Bass
Timpani
Percussion°

°Arranged in a consistent fashion, such as Snare Drum, Bass Drum/Cymbals, Accessory Instruments, Mallet Instruments.

Harp
Piano°

°Followed by other keyboard instruments, such as Celesta, Organ, Accordion, Synthesizer, etc.

Other instruments: Electric Bass, Guitar, Banjo, Electronic Tape, etc.

Stage, Dance, Jazz, or Big Band

1st Alto Saxophone
2nd Alto Saxophone
1st Tenor Saxophone
2nd Tenor Saxophone
Baritone Saxophone°

°Some theater or dance orchestrations use the label Reed 1, Reed 2, etc., for woodwind parts and often require the players to double on additional instruments.

Trumpet 1
Trumpet 2
Trumpet 3
Trumpet 4
Trombone 1
Trombone 2
Trombone 3
Trombone 4 (or Bass Trombone)
Tuba
Piano/Keyboards
Bass
Guitar
Drum Set
Auxiliary Percussion

Property Markings

nvest in a legible property stamp or embosser to use on all your parts and scores. This should show your organization's name. Addresses can change, personnel can change, and phone numbers can change, so confine the extent of the stamp's marking to the name of the organization.

Find a consistently clean space in the music to stamp the individual parts. Make sure the space you choose doesn't interfere with the part number count you will add. This points to the bottom center of the first page of music as the logical choice. Wherever you decide to place your property marking, be consistent.

Be careful that you don't stamp over any notes or that the ink doesn't bleed through to the other side of the paper and obscure any music.

You may also decide to add the set's catalog number to each part for easy reshelving. Only do as much as you think necessary based on the needs of your musicians, your library, and your timeframe.

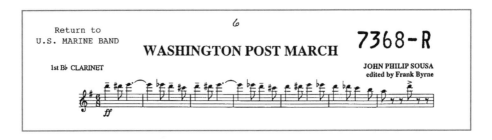

Part with property stamp, part number, and library catalog number.

Numbering Parts

Style

I t's a good idea to determine an in-house style for numbering your parts. Neat and legible numbers will come in handy when breaking down your folders or hunting for that pesky errant part during rehearsals. Try to maintain these two standards in numbering by keeping your numbers:

1. Large
2. Legible

Determine on which side of the page to mark your numbers. Some put string numbers on one side of the page and wind numbers on the opposite. Some put the numbers in a neatly stenciled circle. Others use a rubber stamp for each number. Whatever style you settle upon, be consistent.

Orchestra

STRINGS

String parts are numbered within each section (1st violin, 2nd violin, viola, cello, bass) so that each stand will always get the same part each time the work is played. This way divisi markings and performance notes on that part will always go to the same stand.

Violin I: suppose you have 9 total parts.

- Concertmaster part: mark "1/8"
- 2nd desk, Violin I: mark "2"
- 3rd desk, Violin I: mark "3"

And so on

- 8th desk, Violin I: mark "8/8"

Keep the 9th part unmarked for a clean master just in case

Violin 2, Viola, Cello, Bass: proceed in the same manner

WINDS

Put the parts in score order. (See the article "Score Order.")

- Flute 1: 1/the total number of parts in the wind set, e.g., "1/32"
- Flute 2: mark "2"
- Piccolo: mark "3"

And so on

- Final part: mark "part number" as a fraction over the total number of parts, e.g., "32/32"

In the wind, brass, and percussion set, each unique part should receive a separate number. Duplicate or multiple copies of a given part should all receive the same number, but with a letter added to differentiate each of the multiple copies.

For example, assistant parts receive the same part number as the principal part with the letter "a" following the part number, e.g., Horn 1 = 12, Asst. Horn 1 = 12a.

For percussion parts that have several instruments printed on the same part, give each copy of the same part the same number with a letter added. Therefore, if one percussion part has three different instruments listed—cymbal, bass drum, and bells—you should have copies available for three different players, numbered 23a, 23b, and 23c.[1]

Remember that the number of parts from one composition to the next may be different and therefore the individual parts may be numbered differently between sets. For example, if the 2nd Oboe part in a Beethoven Symphony is number 4 (1st Flute = 1, 2nd Flute = 2, 1st Oboe = 3), in a Mozart Concerto with no flutes, the 2nd Oboe part would be number 2.

Band

Band parts differ from orchestra parts in that there are often multiple players on one part, such as four 1st Flutes and four 2nd Flutes. Follow the same rule that you apply for percussion parts in the orchestra by adding letters to your numerical system. You may decide not to number extra copies of each part if they will not be used for your band's size or instrumentation.

- Piccolo: mark "1/the total number of different parts in the wind set," e.g., "1/32"
- Flute 1, Player 1: mark "2a/however many Flute 1 parts there are," e.g., "2a/d"
- Flute 1, Player 2: mark "2b"
- Flute 1, Player 3: mark "2c"
- Flute 1, Player 4: mark "2d/d" (if last player)
- Flute 2, Player 1: mark "3a/however many Flute 2 parts there are," e.g., "3a/d"
- Flute 2, Player 2: mark "3b"
- Flute 2, Player 3: mark "3c"
- Flute 2, Player 4: mark "3d/d" (if last player)

And so on

- Final part: mark "part number" as a fraction over the total number of parts, e.g., "32/32"

---

1 If you are uncertain how many percussion players are required for a given work, consult one of the books of percussion assignments listed in the Bibliography. A better solution, if possible, is to ask your percussion section leader how many copies of each part is needed for the number of players and the number of instruments.

Choir

Number every choral part and folder consecutively. When assembling your folders, all Part Number 1s will go into Folder number 1 which will be assigned to one person. This makes life easy when breaking down your folders and finding certain numbers missing. For example, if Part number 3 is missing from one of your sets, you can contact the player who signed out Folder number 3.

Scores

Number the scores in the upper left (or right) corner as follows: Copy 1, Copy 2, etc. Be sure to number only exact copies of the same score in this sequence. If you have one Kalmus score and one Bärenreiter score, they each get "Copy 1" because they are different publishers, different editions, different editors, etc., even if they are for the same composition.

Inventory Records

I n addition to numbering your parts, you may decide to keep an inventory sheet listing all the individual parts in a single set of a work. This record will show the number of actual parts. For example, if you own three principal trumpet parts, this would be recorded on the inventory sheet.

Incorporating this form into your loan process will show what is loaned and what you expect to have returned. If you don't have a specific music loan form, you can use a blank copy of your inventory form.

You may keep this inventory with the actual set of parts, stored separately in a binder, in a card catalog, or as a digital computer file.

There are sample inventory forms in the Appendix.

Orchestra Library Inventory

Composer *Beethoven*

Title *Symphony No. 5*   Catalog no. *65*

1 Flute I.	**1** Horn I.	**1** Timpani I.
1 Flute II.	**1** Horn II.	___ Timpani II.
___ Flute III.	___ Horn III.	
___ Flute IV.	___ Horn IV.	___ Percussion
1 Piccolo	___ Horn V.	
	___ Horn VI.	
	___ Horn VII.	
	___ Horn VIII.	
1 Oboe I.		
1 Oboe II.	___ Wagner Tuben I.	
___ Oboe III.	___ Wagner Tuben II.	
___ Oboe IV.	___ Wagnre Tuben III.	
___ English Horn	___ Wagner Tuben IV.	
		___ Harp I.
	1 Trumpet I.	___ Harp II.
1 Clarinet I.	**1** Trumpet II.	
1 Clarinet II.	___ Trumpet III.	___ Piano
___ Clarinet III.	___ Trumpet IV.	___ Celeste
___ Clarinet IV.		___ Organ
___ Eb Clarinet		___ Keyboard I.
___ Bass Clarinet		___ Keyboard II.
	1 Trombone I.	**Strings**
	1 Trombone II.	
1 Bassoon I.	**1** Trombone III.	**8** Violin I.
1 Bassoon II.	___ Trombone IV.	**7** Violin II.
___ Bassoon III.	___ Bass Trombone	**6** Viola
___ Bassoon IV.	___ Euphonium (Tenor Tuba)	**6** Cello
1 Contra Bassoon		**5** Bass
	___ Tuba I.	
___ Soprano Sax	___ Tuba II.	
___ Alto Sax		
___ Tenor Sax		

The Performance Record

t's important to keep an ongoing record of what was performed, not only for historical purposes, but to guide future programming. The library will inevitably receive
the question, "When was the last time we did Brahms 4?" when your administration
is putting together next season's programming. Most institutions try to avoid programming works in back-to-back seasons, with a common rule of thumb being a five-year
moratorium on duplicating works.

Format

There are several options for recording this information, listed below from simple to
more complex:

- Hand-written log housed with the actual set
- A binder of individual sheets devoted to the performance record of individual
  works, filed alphabetically by composer
- Spreadsheet listing
- Database linking catalog records to the performance history

Types of performance records

Internal library records that include:

- List of string principals for bowing history
- Rental/purchase cost history
- Conductor/Soloist-specific edits
  » Cuts
  » Repeats taken or not taken
  » Changes to the actual music
- Errata added
- String count

External records for use by the ensemble's administrative offices:

- Date(s) of concert
- Venue
- Timing
- Conductor
- Soloist(s)
- Perhaps a database hyperlink to the entire program to see what else was played

A sample performance record is included in the Appendix.

PERFORMANCE RECORD			
Beethoven, Symphony No. 5 (Set 1)			
Date	**Ensemble**	**Conductor**	**Event**
January 2011	New set		
February 12, 2011	Bowings added from Philharmonic ; Errata corrected		
March 17, 18, 19, 22, 2011	Orchestra	Bernard Haitink	Subscription concert

Creating a Preservation Set

I f you have rare, fragile, or one-of-a-kind sets of music in your library, you may want to create a preservation or reproduction set of parts in order to keep the originals safe from loss and damage. The preservation set is a useful way to protect unique or high-use materials, such as original manuscripts, custom arrangements, out-of-print editions, or music that is used frequently, including encores or marches in flip folders. This set can also be used to recreate music in an emergency, if a folder is lost or damaged.[2]

A preservation set consists of one copy of each part and a score from a piece of music. Setting these aside, not to be used, ensures that a master copy of every performance part is available for the future.

Candidates for preservation sets include:

- Original compositions in manuscript for which your library is the sole source
- Custom arrangements created for your ensemble
- Music that is frequently used, such as encores, school songs, or march folder pieces
- Music that is out of print and no longer available for sale
- Rare or fragile sets

How to prepare a preservation set

Gather together all copies of the parts for the set of music. Check the music storage folder, all active concert folders, and any standing folders that are kept ready for immediate use.

Compare your collection of parts against your library inventory or the instrumentation list in the score. Make sure that you have at least one copy of every part published. Purchase missing parts or acquire copies from another library to complete your preservation set.

When possible, replace lost or damaged music in your collection by purchasing it from the publisher or a reprint publisher that deals in out-of-print editions. Make photocopies of the parts in your preservation set only when it will not violate copyright laws.

Also be aware that some publishers will make changes in instrumentation or orchestration to different editions or printings of the same music title. Ensure that you don't mix different editions or printings in your preservation set unless they are compatible.

---

2 Keep in mind, however, that if a work is still available for sale or under copyright, it should not be reproduced without the permission of the publisher or the copyright holder. An exception in the copyright law can be made in the following instance: "Emergency copying to replace purchased copies which for any reason are not available for an imminent performance provided purchased replacement copies shall be substituted in due course." ("Reproduction of Copyrighted Works by Educators and Librarians." Circular 21. United States Copyright Office, Washington, D.C., revision 11/2009.)

Select one copy of each part for preservation. Choose parts without performance markings, printer errors, or other disfiguring smudges. A page with good contrast between the ink and the paper will yield better quality photocopies.

Remove all paper clips, staples, and rubber bands from the music. These items will deteriorate over time and stain or damage the paper they touch.

Store your preservation set apart from the other music in the storage folder by placing it inside a separate envelope. Mark this envelope clearly with the music composer, title, catalog number, and the label "preservation set."

Ideally, the envelopes you use should be "acid-free" or preservation quality. That is, they should not be made of materials with a high acid or alkaline content that will harm the music. Storing your preservation set in an acid-free or pH neutral envelope will slow the deterioration of this protected music.

Common envelope sizes for music storage are:

- 6×9 inches for march-size parts
- 9×15 inches for letter or legal paper
- 12×15 inches for larger format editions

Finally, instruct your library staff and others who may have access to your collection (conductors, arrangers, etc.) of the purpose and importance of the preservation set. Stress to them that these preserved parts should never be removed from their protective folder without the supervision of the librarian.

Sources for preservation quality envelopes and supplies

The Hollinger Corporation.
   http://www.hollingermetaledge.com
Gaylord Brothers, Inc.
   http://www.gaylord.com
University Products, Inc.
   http://www.universityproducts.com

Reprint publishers

Bovaco.
   http://bovacomusic.com (Band music from the library of The Detroit Concert
   Band and Leonard B. Smith)
Broude Brothers Limited.
   http://www.broude.us
Edwin F. Kalmus & Co., Inc.
   http://www.kalmus-music.com
Luck's Music Library.
   http://www.lucksmusic.com
Masters Music Publications & Ludwig Masters Publications.
   http://www.masters-music.com
Subito Music Corporation.
   http://www.subitomusic.com

Processing checklist

Processing includes adding the music to your collection and preparing it for use by the musicians. These steps will help protect your investment and standardize the manner in which your music is organized and housed.

_____ 1. Arrange your set of parts in score order. See the article:

- *Score Order*

_____ 2. Mark the music to identify it as your property. See the article:

- *Property Markings*

_____ 3. Number the parts. See the article:

- *Numbering Parts*

_____ 4. Prepare an inventory sheet describing and itemizing each part in the set. See the article:

- *Inventory Records*

_____ 5. Prepare a performance record sheet that will document the use of the music as well as any work done to the set as a result of the performances. See the article:

- *The Performance Record*

_____ 6. Prepare a folder or container that will house the parts when they are stored on the shelf. See the article:

- *Library Supplies and Equipment*

_____ 7. Take any steps necessary to protect and preserve the music in your collection. See the article:

- *Creating a Preservation Set*

Reproducible forms to assist with processing are available in the Appendix.

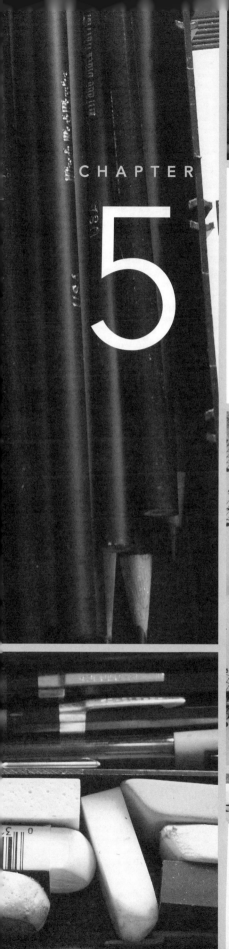

5

MUSIC
PREPARATION

How to Mark Parts

Bowings

Typically, the performance library is responsible for adding bowings to all orchestra music that is signed out for performances, readings, or recordings. This type of work requires good music notation skills, clear and consistent handwriting, and above all, attention to detail.

Use the first stand part in each string section as the master. It should show the bowings for all parts in the section, including all divisi passages. This will allow the principal player to know the markings for each player in their section. The bowmarkers should also use this part to copy the markings for the rest of the section. Also, if you make practice photocopies for the players, use this part as a master because it will show the markings for every player on each stand, regardless of where they are sitting.

Check the part over before giving it to the bowmarkers to make sure the markings are clear and legible and a good model for the bowmarkers to copy. Remember that in some works the first stand part may have so many solo passages that it will be more convenient to use the second stand part as the bowing master.

Following are some suggestions for marking clear, clean, and legible bowings for both librarians and bowmarkers:

- Make the bowings look like the music notation used in the part, both in size and style, so they don't distract the player's eye.
- Place the bow markings above the staff, centered over the note head, unless other markings are in the way. In that case, mark them as close to the appropriate note as possible.
- Try not to obscure any printed musical instructions, such as expression markings and dynamics.
- Unless otherwise instructed, copy *all* markings from the first stand part into the rest of the section. This includes bowings, slurs, articulation markings, written instructions, and page turn aids.
- If some existing markings are correct but sloppy or illegible, erase and recopy them neatly.
- Feel free (within reason) to "color in" faded barlines, staff lines, and cracked or incomplete notes to make the part more readable.
- When cleaning up the parts, erase all unessential information added by the previous players, such as eyeglasses, arrows, circles, or other markings that would interfere with reading the music. Also remove phone numbers, messages between players, and caricatures of the conductor.

There are several books on bowing technique and practice in the bibliography at the end of this article. Be sure to also read the article on "Music Notation Guidelines" and the books in that bibliography to familiarize yourself with the rules and practices of music notation.

Examples

These markings are irregular and inconsistent in shape and size.

These are more consistent and proportional in size to the notation.

Draw slurs from the center of one note head to the other, in a graceful arc. Center any expression marks (like the staccato dots and the accent mark) directly over or under the note head.

These slurs clearly show changes made to the printed markings.

Any writing on the parts (measure numbers, dynamics, instructions) should be legible and easy to read.

When you are finished, give the music one last look. It's not necessary to proof-read every mark and bowing—paying attention when doing the work will help prevent most errors—but look at every page of each part to be sure you didn't skip a page or overlook something (adding measure numbers, for example).

Mark a part at a time or a page at a time?

Everyone has their own preference for how they mark a set of parts. The two options are to copy all markings throughout the section a page at a time, or to bow one entire part straight through, then move onto the next part. Some professional librarians prefer the first method, particularly for complex pieces, because they can focus their attention on smaller segments and ensure that each bowing, slur, and articulation is copied reliably from page to page. There are advantages to both systems, but the most important issue is to be neat, consistent, and accurate.

Xs in the margins

In major orchestras, the library staff is responsible for marking bowing changes that occur during rehearsal. The principal players mark an "X" in the outer margin of each stave or system that has a change. This immediately shows the librarians those passages that need correction so they don't waste time checking through the entire part.

Following rehearsal, the librarians collect the folders, find the Xs in the 1st stand part, and make sure that those changes are marked in each part throughout that section. The last step is to erase the Xs from the first stand part so the player knows the correction has been made and so the librarians don't waste time looking at old Xs the next time they check bowings.

Cleaning and remarking parts

Some rental sets may arrive heavily marked with sloppy bowings, phrasings, and extraneous comments. When cleaning up these sets, use the Golden Rule of Part Preparation: If a marking is too messy to decipher or is something you would not want to see on your own part—fix it!

For example, erase:

- Fingerings, because they tend to be personal to the player
- Unnecessary comments such as "count" or "listen to Pierre"
- Drawings, pictures, or tic-tac-toe games

But leave:

- Neatly written cues, identified by instrument ("listen to clarinet")
- Corrected notes or other errata

BEFORE

AFTER

Annotated bibliography

Berman, Joel, Barbara G. Jackson, and Kenneth Sarch. *Dictionary of Bowing and Pizzicato Terms*. 4th ed. Bloomington, Ind.: Tichenor Publishing, 1999.

This is a detailed and well-illustrated explanation of bowing techniques, effects, and styles set in a dictionary format.

Galamian, Ivan. *Principles of Violin Playing & Teaching*. Englewood Cliffs, N.J.: Prentice-Hall, 1985.

A string instrument instruction manual with notated examples of bowing principles and techniques.

Gigante, Charles. *Manual of Orchestral Bowing*. Bloomington, Ind.: Frangipani Press, 1986.

A publication of the American String Teachers Association. Part 1 introduces the basic principals of bowing technique and Part 2 identifies bowing styles with many examples from the orchestral repertoire.

Green, Elizabeth A. H. *The Dynamic Orchestra: Principles of Orchestral Performance for Instrumentalists, Conductors, and Audiences*. Englewood Cliffs, N.J.: Prentice-Hall, 1987.

Chapter Six discusses "Bowing Principles," outlining the author's concepts on musical and technical bowing decisions, with her suggestions for marking bowings in parts.

———. *Orchestral Bowings and Routines*. 2nd ed. Ann Arbor, Mich.: Campus Publishers, 1957.

A pedagogical manual outlining the basic concepts for determining bowings in orchestral works.

Rabin, Marvin, and Priscilla Smith. *Guide to Orchestral Bowings Through Musical Styles*. Rev. ed. Madison: University of Wisconsin-Madison, 1990.

This manual and the companion videotape demonstrate bow movement and technique in different musical styles.

Divisi Markings

The term *divisi* indicates that a musical line is to be divided into two or more parts, to be performed by separate players. As it applies to the string instruments, it shows how the players in the section divide up to cover all the musical lines. For multiple or complex divisi, this ensures that the voices are divided equally through the section.

The first stand part for each section should show the bowings for all lines and all staves. This way the principal player will know all the bowings for their section and the bowmarker can use this part to mark any stand in that section. The librarian (or possibly the section leader) should mark the divisi assignments in each stand's part to indicate which lines the players should follow. Mark the appropriate lines with pencil hash marks in the left margin, one line for each player. The bowmarkers should bow only those lines that have hash marks.

First stand with all parts bowed

Second stand with only that stave bowed

Most two-part divisi (divisi by 2 at the stand—see example below) are typically not marked because the players will know from experience that the upper stave is played by the outside player and the lower stave is played by the inside player. In these cases, both staves should be bowed because both will be played.

If a divisi pattern repeats from system to system, only the first system on the page may need to be marked as it is intended that the pattern will continue until a change in divisi assignments is indicated.

If a passage is intended for only one or just a few players, mark the other stands with parentheses or brackets to show that the remaining players are tacet for that passage. These passages should be bowed for only those stands that actually play the passage.

Some works have complex and confusing divisi passages that move from line to line, sometimes within a system. These may be unique to each stand and the player's lines should be indicated with hash marks and arrows to show where their part moves. Notate these markings clearly to indicate that all the appropriate passages are bowed and played.

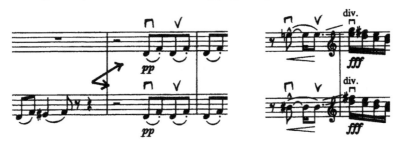

It may be most efficient to first mark all the parts in the section to show divisi, tacet, and other unusual passages for each stand, working through the section a part at a time. This way, when you begin bowing, all that you (or your bowmarkers) have to do is follow the divisi indications and add the bowings, dynamics, and performance instructions for the appropriate stand. If a conductor or section leader has marked these divisi responsibilities, don't erase or change the markings without asking.

There are three forms of divisi playing:

- By player, also known as "divisi at the stand" or "at the desk," with each player on the stand taking a separate line. For example, with a two line divisi, all the outside players play the top line while all the inside players play the bottom line. (See example below.)
- By stand, also known as "divisi by stands," with both players on the stand playing the same line and the lines alternating by stands throughout the section. For example, with a two line divisi, stands 1, 3, 5, and 7 will play the top line while stands 2, 4, 6, and 8 play the bottom line. (See example below.)
- By group within the section, with the assignments divided to apportion the parts equally. For example, with a two line divisi, the front stands (1, 2, 3, and 4) play the upper line and the back stands (5, 6, 7, and 8) play the lower line. An example can be seen in the first violin section divisi in Richard Strauss's *Also Sprach Zarathustra*.

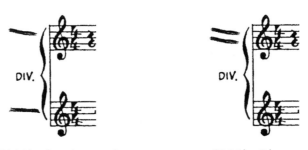

Divisi by 2 at the stand   Divisi by 2 by stands

Sections divided by 3 are usually divided by stand or at the stand. The assignments will rotate throughout the section and repeat after every group of three stands.

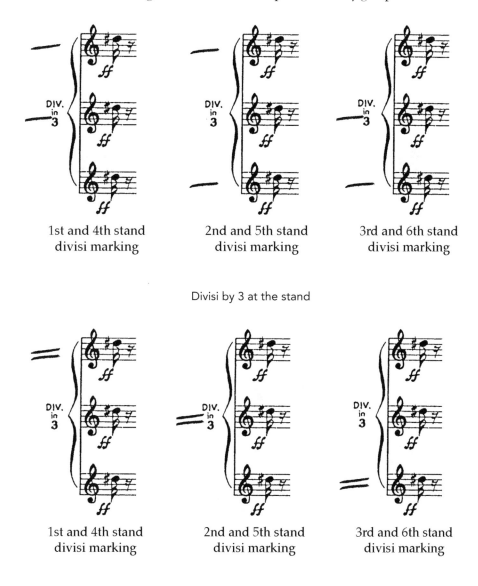

1st and 4th stand divisi marking	2nd and 5th stand divisi marking	3rd and 6th stand divisi marking

Divisi by 3 at the stand

1st and 4th stand divisi marking	2nd and 5th stand divisi marking	3rd and 6th stand divisi marking

Divisi by 3 by stands

Divisi of four or more stands or players will be marked in a similar fashion, according to the number of lines or staves to divide and the number of players in the section. An extreme example is Penderecki's *Threnody to the Victims of Hiroshima*, which divides the violins into twenty-four parts, the violas and cellos into ten parts, and the basses into eight parts.

If a passage is divided into lines for a soloist (or soloists) and the rest of the section, the solo line is marked for those players and the other lines (identified as *gli altri* in Italian, *die Übrigen* in German, and *les autres* in French) are marked for the rest of the section.

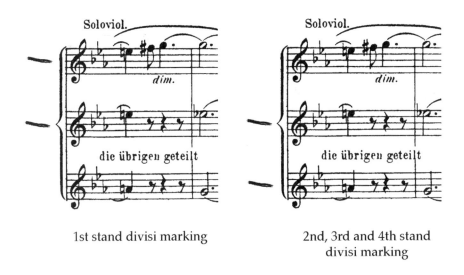

1st stand divisi marking   2nd, 3rd and 4th stand
                                      divisi marking

Terms identifying divisi passages:

divisi (It.) abbreviated as div.
geteilt (Ger.) abbreviated as get. or geth.
la metà (It.) = at the half; i.e., half the section plays
die Hälfte (Ger.) = at the half; i.e., half the section plays
la moitié (Fr.) = at the half; i.e., half the section plays
en trois parties (Fr.) = divisi by 3
dreifach geteilt (Ger.) = divisi by 3
pultweise geteilt (Ger.) = divisi by stand; i.e., Stand 1 plays the upper line, Stand 2 plays the lower line, etc. Note that there is some confusion about this term and you should consult the concertmaster or conductor to be sure the section is divided as they expect.

Terms canceling divisi passages:

unison (Eng.)	tutti (It.)	unisson (Fr.)
non div. (Eng., used by Bartók)	unisoni (It.)	
alle (Ger.)	zusammen (Ger.)	

Performance Aids for the Player

P erformance aids are markings added by the librarian as a courtesy to make a part more readable or more functional for the player. These can include markings that some players may make themselves, but by standardizing them throughout the part or section, it ensures that all players are informed.

For example, fill in any "broken notes" that didn't print correctly and darken staff or stem lines that are faded and hard to read.

Before   After

Include page turn hints, such as "V.S." (volti subito [It.] = turn quickly) where appropriate. Also write in the number of measures rest on the previous or the following pages to help the player count through the turn.

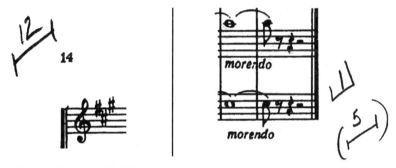

For wind parts that have doublings—two or more instruments played by a single player (e.g., Flute doubling on Piccolo or Oboe doubling on English Horn)—make sure these instrument changes are marked in two places:

- Write "to English Horn" (or Piccolo or whatever) immediately after the last notes played before the change so the player has time to pick up and prepare the instrument
- Write the instrument name immediately before or at the next entrance to remind the player of the change

The same courtesy could be extended to mute changes for brass and string parts.

Terms that indicate a change to another instrument or (sometimes) a tuning change:

muta, muta in (It.)	
changez, changez en (Fr.)	prenez, prendre (Fr.)
umstimmen nach (Ger.)	vorbereiten (Ger.)

Cuts

A cut in the music tells the player to move from one point to another by skipping over musical material that will not be performed. Cuts must be marked legibly, efficiently, and above all, accurately to avoid confusion and error.

Mark the beginning of the cut with a thick vertical line extending above and below the staff. Mark the end of the cut with a second vertical line and connect the two with a line to show the linear progression of the cut.

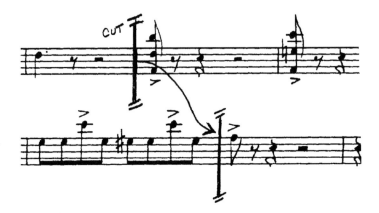

For clarity, write the word "cut" before or above the beginning cut line. A more traditional method divides the word "vide" with the letters "vi—" written at the beginning of the cut and "—de" at the end of the cut to show where the music continues.

The cut marks should be easy for the player to read and follow at a glance. Try not to cover or write over notes or musical instructions when marking the cut. Avoid needless marking on the page or crossing out of the deleted music in case the cut is later erased to restore the passage.

If possible, mark the cut at the same place, the same measure, the same beat, in each part. The location of the cut can then be used as a rehearsal reference point.

Cuts and page turns

If the cut runs across one or more pages, be sure to consider if there is time for the player to make the page turn and continue playing. If not, fix the page turn accordingly. If necessary, photocopy and paste music before or after the cut to accommodate a convenient page turn.

When photocopying to fix a turn, try to keep an indication of where the cut begins and ends visible so the player knows that the music has been altered. Alternatively, write "(cut)" at the point where the two sections of music rejoin to indicate that material has been removed from the part.

Cuts and missing information

Be sure to examine the music in the cut (which will not be played) for any musical changes that will affect the music after the cut, such as:

- Tempo indication
- Key signature
- Meter signature
- Clef change
- Transposition change
- Mute instructions
- Changes to another instrument

Indicate these changes either before or after the cut to show the player this information when they begin to play again.

In the example below, the part is for Bass Clarinet and Basset Horn. The orchestra will take a cut from rehearsal 227 to 246.

The cut spans two facing pages, so the line of the cut would run from the beginning (Vi–) on one page across to the end (–de) on the following page.

In the music that is cut, the player is supposed to change to Basset Horn, so they need to be playing that instrument at their first entrance after the cut (rehearsal 247). Be sure that instrument change is noted as soon as possible.

There is also a meter change in the music that was cut. This is now handwritten in the part so the player sees it immediately where the music resumes. There were also key changes and tempo changes in the music that was cut, but those are notated in the music at rehearsal 246 and already appear in the part.

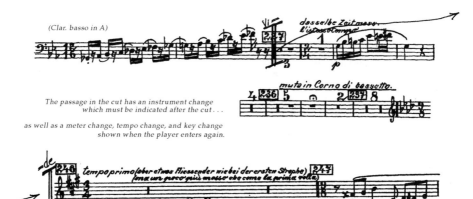

Rehearsal Figures

Rehearsing music that lacks some kind of rehearsal system is a prescription for wasted time and frustrated musicians. Similarly, if the rehearsal figures between the score and the parts are at odds, common ground between the podium and the players will be elusive.

Typical rehearsal systems use either:

- Letters or numbers, placed at significant structural points in the work
- Measure numbers, also known as "bar count"
- A combination of the two

Of the choices above, the third is the most efficient for a work that will receive intense rehearsal. Measure numbers can pinpoint exactly where a problem is occurring and are the most precise method of communication. Rehearsal letters or numbers are helpful as convenient starting points that can be found quickly and communicated easily.

The following are suggestions for applying each to a composition, either a new work about to be printed, or an older work that lacks any rehearsal system altogether. If you have an item that is already numbered (either the score or the parts), follow the numbering system that is already established in that item so the rehearsal figures are consistent throughout the set.

Letters or numbers

Choose significant structural points in the music to place the rehearsal figure: key changes, meter changes, thematic entrances or statements, musical form divisions (exposition, development, variations, etc.).

The figures should be no more than twenty to thirty measures apart so the players don't have to search too far to find a starting point. Conversely, don't place the figures too close together (two to ten measures apart) as the extra marks can clutter the page and become redundant.

Print the rehearsal figure above the staff, set in bold face type, in a size that can be identified easily.

The figure could also be placed inside a circle or a box to set it apart from other text that also appears on the page (Example 1). In the parts, place the figure above the staff so it won't collide with notes, articulations, or bowing.

Example 1. Rehearsal figure in box. Measure numbers at upper left edge of system.

In the score, place the figure above the top staff and also above the 1st Violin staff (Example 2). It can also be placed below the bottom staff if the score is oversize.

Example 2. Rehearsal figures in the full score.

Instead of letters, some composers use the appropriate measure number as the rehearsal figure (Example 3).

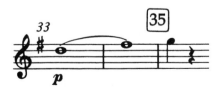

Example 3. Measure numbers as rehearsal figures.

Measure numbers

Write the numbers simply and legibly, without flourish, so they can be read easily. Use a black ink pen so the numbers won't be erased accidentally when cleaning or rebowing the parts.

In the parts, place the numbers in the left margin of each staff or staff system, either centered to the left of the staff or on the upper left edge of the staff itself (Example 4).

Example 4. Measure numbers in the left margins.

In scores, place the numbers at the top left corner of the system on each page. If the score is divided on the page, place the number in the left corner of each division (Example 5).

Example 5. Measure numbers at the start of each score system.

It is not necessary to number each measure of the work, as the extra numbers will clutter the page and get in the way of other markings. However, some copyists who specialize in music for film, theater, and recording studios (where time is money) number each measure for more efficient and precise communication.

Avoid placing measure numbers at fixed distance, e.g., every five measures (used by Creston and Schuman) or every ten measures (used in Eulenberg study scores) for two reasons. First, these numbers rarely occur at a significant structural point in the music, which can make it an awkward place to start playing. Second, it is more efficient if the number is always in the same location on each page or each system, so the player will always know where to look for it.

If a part has several lengthy rests within a system, include the measure number at the beginning of each rest to show how the numbers progress (Example 6).

Example 6. Measure numbers added after long rests.

First and second endings

Publishers may number repeated endings in different ways. Some number each measure individually (Example 7), while others assign one number to the entire ending (Example 8).

Example 7. Numbering each measure in a repeat.

Example 8. Numbering the entire repeat.

If you have an item that is already numbered (either the score or the parts), follow the numbering system that is already established in that item so the numbering is consistent throughout the set.

Counting measures

An easy way to count long periods of rest is as follows: Add the number of measures rest to the measure number at the start of the rest to get the number of the following measure (Example 9).

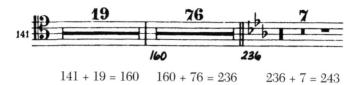

$$141 + 19 = 160 \qquad 160 + 76 = 236 \qquad 236 + 7 = 243$$

Example 9. Counting measures of rest.

Do not count partial measures, such as pick-up notes or measures split between two systems (Example 10), unless they are counted that way in the score or part that you are copying from.

Example 10. Ignore measures with pickups.

When numbering an entire work, create a "crib sheet" that shows significant landmarks in the music and the corresponding measure number. This will help keep you on track as you count through the work and mark the measures.

Schumann: Piano Concerto in A minor, Op. 54
Mvt. I: Allegro affettuoso

measure	event
42	A
67	*Animato*
111	B
156	*Andante espressivo*
185	C (Tempo I. *Allegro*)
205	*Più animato*
259	D (Tempo I. Tutti)
312	*a tempo* (key change)
320	E (*Animato*)
365	F (*a tempo, animato*)
389	total

Music Notation Guidelines

The performance librarian should be familiar with proper music notation because it is one of the languages used in the course of your daily work. It is essential when marking bowings and other performance instructions, correcting errata, reading scores, and communicating with other musicians. The librarian should be an expert on this subject, particularly if you are required to consult with composers who may be unfamiliar with writing for your ensemble. It may also be your responsibility to advise on commissions and communicate the standards expected of these new works.

Knowledge of computer notation software is valuable if you need to create inserts or new parts, but having good hand manuscript skills are vital, especially if a part needs to be fixed in short order.

Strive to make your notation neat and accurate. If you are writing in a published part, use those printed markings as models so that your notation matches that same style and appearance. Your hand notation should not distract from the player's reading or interpretation of the music.

Use quality writing materials for music writing, including black ink pens with different tip sizes and a small ruler for drawing straight lines.

Some general notation guidelines are presented below. You may have to bend these rules on occasion to make your added marking fit into a printed part, but always do your best to make your music writing clear and legible.

- The note head shape is oval, not round
- The accidentals have a diagonal slant and are placed directly in front of the note they affect
- Single note stems are exactly one octave in length

When the note heads are on ledger lines, the stem must reach the middle line of the staff, regardless of the pitch of the note

The beginning of a work should include these elements in this order:
1. Clef sign
2. Key signature
3. Meter signature

Tempo indications
- Marked in bold type with the first word capitalized
- Located above the staff, with the left edge marking the beginning of the new tempo

Modifying terms
- Marked in *italic* type
- Located underneath the staff
examples: *cresc., dim., poco a poco*

Playing instructions
- Marked in roman type
- Located above the staff
  examples: pizz., tacet, arco, tip of the bow

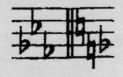

Key Change
- Located after thin double bar lines.
- Cancel the previous accidentals (as appropriate) first before indicating the new key signature

Articulations

Staccato
- Centered on the note head side
- It may be inside the staff in the middle of a space, but should sit between the note and the slur

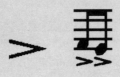

Accent
- Centered on the note head side
- It should remain outside the staff and outside the slur (Older notation styles allowed them inside the slur)

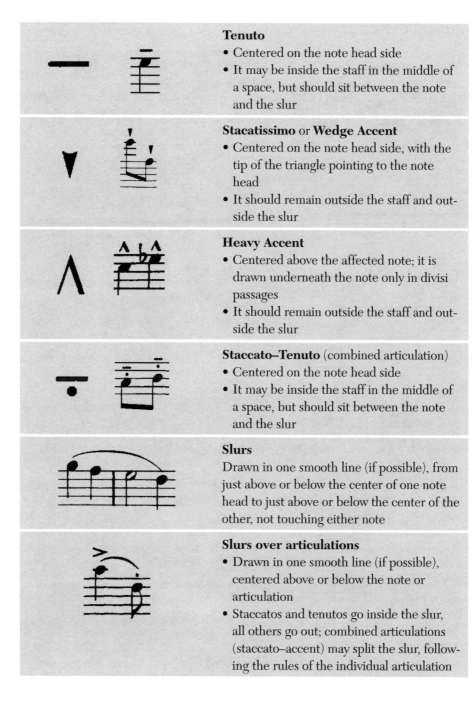

Tenuto
- Centered on the note head side
- It may be inside the staff in the middle of a space, but should sit between the note and the slur

Stacatissimo or **Wedge Accent**
- Centered on the note head side, with the tip of the triangle pointing to the note head
- It should remain outside the staff and outside the slur

Heavy Accent
- Centered above the affected note; it is drawn underneath the note only in divisi passages
- It should remain outside the staff and outside the slur

Staccato–Tenuto (combined articulation)
- Centered on the note head side
- It may be inside the staff in the middle of a space, but should sit between the note and the slur

Slurs
Drawn in one smooth line (if possible), from just above or below the center of one note head to just above or below the center of the other, not touching either note

Slurs over articulations
- Drawn in one smooth line (if possible), centered above or below the note or articulation
- Staccatos and tenutos go inside the slur, all others go out; combined articulations (staccato–accent) may split the slur, following the rules of the individual articulation

Musical markings

Dynamic markings
- Marked in bold italic type
- Located below the staff and directly under or slightly before the notes they affect

examples: *fff*   *mp*   *pp*

Dynamic accents
- Marked in bold-italic type
- Located directly below the note they affect

examples: *fz*   *sffz*   *sfz*

Fermata
- Centered above the affected note or rest

Down bow — Up bow
- Centered above the affected note
- They may be written below the note in divisi passages

Breath Mark
Located above the staff, between notes to be separated

Caesura
Located between the notes to be separated, extending from the 4th line of the staff up at a 60-degree angle for approximately two spaces (to the 1st ledger line)

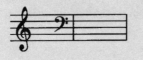

Clef change
Placed before the bar line of the next affected measure, or within the measure before the next affected beat

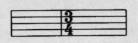

Meter change
Placed after the bar line of the affected measure

Annotated bibliography of music notation manuals

Broido, Arnold, and Daniel Dorff. "Standard Music Notation Practice." New York: Music Publishers' Association, 1993.

A handy booklet describing the basics of music notation. A joint publication of the Music Publishers' Association and the Music Educators National Conference, it is available online at http://mpa.org/music_notation.

Del Mar, Norman. *Anatomy of the Orchestra.* Berkeley, Los Angeles: University of California Press, 1981.

Del Mar describes the organization, arrangement, and performance practice of the modern symphony orchestra. Each section examines an instrumental family (strings, woodwinds, etc.) and outlines typical ranges, their appearance in the score, notation and layout in the parts, and typical or unusual effects. The many musical examples are taken from the orchestral literature.

Gerou, Tom, and Linda Lusk. *Essential Dictionary of Music Notation.* Los Angeles: Alfred Publishing, 1996.

A pocket guide and ready reference manual, arranged in dictionary form, defining music notation terminology and illustrating standard notation practice.

Gould, Elaine. *Behind Bars: The Definitive Guide to Music Notation.* Harlow, England: Faber Music, 2011.

Written by an editor at Faber Music, this rule manual for music notation includes over 1,500 musical examples, but also discusses page formatting and layout for parts and score

Major Orchestra Librarians' Association. "Music Preparation Guidelines for Orchestral Music." n.p.: Major Orchestra Librarians' Association, 2006.

This pamphlet presents guidelines for the proper engraving and formatting of scores and parts. Available online at http://www.mola-inc.org/MOLA%20Guidelines%20Text.htm.

Nicholl, Matthew, and Richard Grudzinski. *Music Notation: Preparing Scores and Parts.* Boston, Mass.: Berklee Press, 2007.

These instructions cover both hand and computer notation practices, with additional instructions for proofreading, copying, binding, and taping parts and scores.

Powell, Steven. *Music Engraving Today: The Art and Practice of Digital Notesetting.* 2nd ed. New York: Brichtmark Music, 2007.

A modern counterpart to the Ross manual (below), focusing on the computer software notation programs Finale and Sibelius. It has invaluable information on notation rules and practice for every copyist and desktop music publisher.

Read, Gardner. *Music Notation: A Manual of Modern Practice*. 2nd ed. New York: Crescendo, 1969.

Detailed explanations and examples of traditional notation, with chapters on instrumental, jazz, and vocal music. Part IV covers manuscript writing, proofreading, and preparing a score and parts.

Risatti, Howard. *New Music Vocabulary: A Guide to Notational Signs for Contemporary Music*. Urbana: University of Illinois Press, 1975.

Illustrates a wide variety of staff and graphic notation, pictographs, and instructions, each used in a contemporary work. The items are classed by instrument family or general use, with an index to reference the desired effects.

Ross, Ted. *The Art of Music Engraving and Processing: A Complete Manual, Reference and Text Book on Preparing Music for Reproduction and Print*. 2nd ed. Miami, Fla.: Charles Hansen, 1970.

This manual describes the process of engraving music manuscript, explaining in detail the rules of notation applied to professional music printing. A CD-ROM version is published by NPC Imaging (http://www.npcimaging.com).

Solomon, Samuel Z. *How to Write for Percussion: A Comprehensive Guide to Percussion Composition*. New York, N.Y.: SZSolomon, 2002.

An illustrated manual of percussion notation with many photographs, charts, and musical examples that show contemporary percussion performance practice and technique.

Stone, Kurt. *Music Notation in the Twentieth Century: A Practical Guidebook*. New York: W. W. Norton, 1980.

A textbook describing contemporary notation, written in two parts, covering: 1) general conventions of notation, pitch, duration, score and parts, rhythm, and indeterminate events, and 2) specific notation for instruments including keyboard reductions, voice, and taped sound.

Binding Music for Performance

B inding music for performance has different requirements than music used for study and scholarship. Performance parts must lie flat when opened. The notes must be large enough for a player to read on a music stand from a distance of two to three feet and, in the case of string section parts, to be read by two players sharing a single stand. The music paper should be of sufficient weight to remain upright on the stand and sturdy enough to withstand repeated writing and erasing of bowing marks and performance notes.

Most parts from publishers are bound well enough to use without additional work. On occasion, rental parts will need repair, purchased parts will need reformatting to improve page turns, and new compositions will need to have parts created. The librarian should know how to prepare a good performance part and also be able to advise composers and copyists on music preparation issues. Some binding techniques commonly used in performance library collections are described below.

The terminology used is taken from the publishing industry. The individual sheets of paper that make up a part are referred to as leaves. A page is one side of a leaf. The front of the leaf, the side that lies to the right in an open part, is called the recto-page (or simply recto). The back of the leaf, the side that lies to the left when the leaf is turned, is called the verso. Rectos are odd-numbered pages; versos are even numbered pages.[1]

Parts bound in signatures

A signature is a printed sheet folded one or more times. This creates multiple pages. Most published parts consist of one or more signatures, gathered together, trimmed, and bound at the spine.

A part made up of signatures can also be created from single leaves. For example, six single leaves with music printed on both sides, when taped together to form signatures, will yield a part of twelve pages total. To create a signature-bound part in this manner, arrange the single leaves so that the first leaf (pages 1 and 2) lays on the right and the last leaf (pages 11 and 12) lays on the left. Their inside margins should touch along the long vertical edge (Example 1). Tape the two leaves together along the long edge using flexible cloth tape or another sturdy, yet flexible tape product, such as Filmoplast, hinge repair tape,[2] or even adhesive tape, if a better product is unavailable. Fold the leaves together so that the taped spine is on the outside of the fold. Tape the next two leaves in the same manner (pages 3 and 4 and pages 9 and 10)

This information first appeared, in part, in *A Manual for the Performance Library* by Russ Girsberger (Music Library Association Basic Manual Series, no. 6. Lanham, Md.: Scarecrow Press, 2006).

1   *The Chicago Manual of Style* (15th ed. Chicago: University of Chicago Press, 2003), 4.

2   For suggestions and sources of binding equipment, see the article on "Library Supplies and Equipment."

until all leaves are paired up and taped. Insert each set of taped leaves inside the other to create a part of made of three 4-page signatures (Example 2).

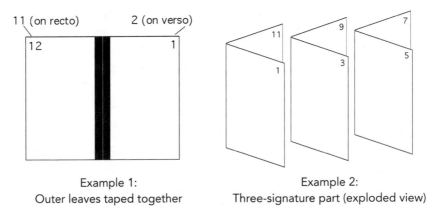

Example 1:
Outer leaves taped together

Example 2:
Three-signature part (exploded view)

Bind the signatures together by sewing or saddle-stapling from the outside of the spine into the folded sheets. The part should lay flat when opened and be sturdy enough for use in performance.[3]

If a single loose leaf must be added to a bound part, place it in position aligned with the other leaves. Using flexible cloth tape, affix the leaf to a signature, taping the left margin of the recto onto the adjacent signature. If necessary, remove the binding stitches or staples to make the leaf lay properly in the part, then rebind the part. Trim the inserted leaf to match the size of the other leaves.

Parts bound with tape

Example 3:
Fanned single sheets

Single sheet parts may also be bound together using flexible cloth tape. Given a part made up of single sheets with music printed on both sides, arrange the sheets in order by page number. Fan the pages, leaving a small strip of the left margin of each recto visible (Example 3). Lay a strip of flexible cloth tape over the left margin of the sheets so that the right half of the tape touches each of the pages. Press the tape down firmly onto the sheets with your thumb or a bone folder so it adheres securely. Fold the left half of the tape over onto the verso of the last leaf. The tape will adhere to the exposed margins of each leaf, securing them in the spine of the part. The flexible cloth tape allows each page to lay flat while it remains attached to the taped spine.

---

3   Instructions on how to sew bindings can be found at this website, sponsored by the Indiana University libraries: http://www.indiana.edu/~libpres/manual/manintro.html.

Accordion-fold parts

Accordion-fold or fan-fold parts are single-sided sheets of paper taped together in order, side by side on the long edge. These parts can be unwieldy on the stand and while they may not always solve the issue of page turns, they sometimes allow the player more flexibility to arrange their own turns. If an accordion-fold binding must be used because of player needs or performance set-up, format the part as follows for maximum efficiency and stability.

Use at least 70 lb. offset or a similar weight paper. Attach the pages using flexible cloth tape, hinge binding tape, or adhesive tape. Always join the pages with the taped spine on the outside of the fold; that is, when the pages are folded, the taped spine is visible. Folding pages with the taped spine on the inside of the fold creates a gap between the pages where sticky tape is visible and likely to attach itself to other pages and parts.

To create an accordion-fold part, begin with single sheets of music, copied on one side only. Lay pages 1 and 2 side by side, face up, touching along the long vertical edge. Place a heavy object (stapler, book, or other item) in the middle of each page to hold the paper in position. Attach the two pages with a vertical strip of tape on the long edge where they meet. Fold and crease the pages to be sure the tape adheres to the paper. Trim any excess tape from the top and bottom of the page.

Next, lay the taped pages 1 and 2 face down on the right and lay page 3 face down on the left. Attach page 3 to page 2 with a vertical strip of tape along the back of the part. Fold the pages so the tape is on the outside of the fold and crease them to be sure the tape adheres to the paper. Trim any excess tape from the top and bottom of the page.

Flip the three taped pages over so they are face up and lay page 4 face up to the right of the taped pages. Tape page 4 to page 3 with a vertical strip of tape, as before. Fold and crease the pages to be sure the tape adheres to the paper. Trim any excess tape from the top and bottom of the page. Continue in a similar fashion until all pages in the part are taped together (Example 4). Assembling the part can be done in any order that is convenient, such as all the face up pages first (1 to 2, 3 to 4, 5 to 6), then all the face down pages (2 to 3, 4 to 5, 6 to 7).

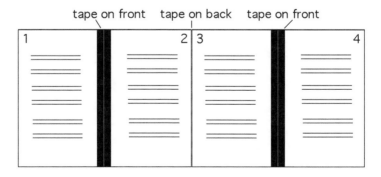

Example 4: Fan-folded pages

The instructions above work for flexible cloth tape and hinge tape. If you use adhesive tape, first lay a 2-inch long strip of tape horizontally across the top edge of the pages to attach them. Add a second strip across the bottom edge of the pages. This not only holds the pages in place for taping, but gives additional security against tears at the seam. Lay one long strip of tape vertically on the long edges where the pages meet, so it attaches to the tape strips at the top and bottom of the page. Trim any excess and fold and crease the pages to be sure the tape adheres to the paper.

Binding scores

Some conductor's scores, vocal scores, or performance parts may be too large for tape binding to be efficient. These materials may still be bound in-house using either a plastic spiral coil or a comb binding system. These binding machines are available from several manufacturers. (See the article "Library Supplies and Equipment.") Choose a machine that will accommodate large format materials with a binding edge ranging from 11 to 17 inches. Of the two systems, the spiral coil binding tends to lay better on the stand with less noise when turning pages. Plastic combs can crack and break as they age and may cause more friction and noise as the pages are tuned. Commercial printers and photocopy businesses also offer these bindings if your library can afford to outsource this work.

For case bound (hard-cover) binding, contact a local book bindery. Academic performance libraries may be able to submit binding work through their school's library contract. More information on this type of binding can be found in Alice Carli's manual.[4]

---

4   Alice Carli, *Binding and Care of Printed Music* (Music Library Association Basic Manual Series, no. 2. Lanham, Md.: Scarecrow Press, 2003).

Fixing Page Turns

Poor layout that forces the musician to turn a page while playing should be avoided at all costs. Composers and publishers should be aware of this issue when printing music, but they may not always address it. When the librarian or player is confronted with awkward page layout, there are several creative solutions to the problem:

- Look several measures before and after the turn to find a multi-measure or multi-beat rest that would allow a convenient page turn. Photocopy the intervening measure, measures, or system of music and tape it to the bottom of the previous or the top of the following page, where appropriate.

If necessary, the photocopied measures could be reduced slightly to fit in the space available. Be sure to identify or delete the music that has been copied so the player does not repeat the duplicated passage, and if necessary, show the player where to begin playing again after the turn.

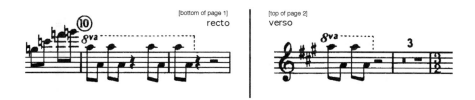

Example 1: Page turn before

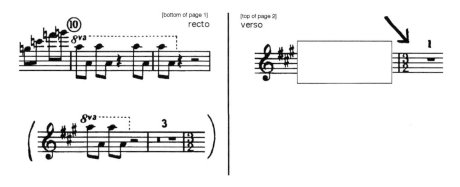

Example 2: Page turn after

Example 1 shows the bottom of page 1 (recto) and the top of page 2 (verso). The notes continue without pause, causing the player to turn the page while playing. If the publisher had placed the turn on page 1 just one measure later, the player would have had plenty of time to turn the page and prepare to continue playing. Example 2 shows a measure of notes and a three-measure rest copied and taped at the bottom of page 1, so the player can finish the phrase and have time to turn. The copied passage on the top of page 2 is covered up with a piece of paper and the arrow indicates where the player should continue to play after the turn.

- If the only convenient place to turn a page is many staves from the end of the page, photocopy an entire leaf and tape it to the edge of the music to create a three or four-page spread.

In the example below, the music at the bottom of page 3 continued onto page 4 (verso of 3) with no pause, creating an impossible page turn. There is time, however, to turn during a six measure rest at the bottom of page 4. The solution is to photocopy page 4 and tape it to the right edge of page 3 to create a three-page spread (Example 3). This will allow the musician to play continually from the top of page 2 to the bottom of page 4 without worrying about an awkward page turn.

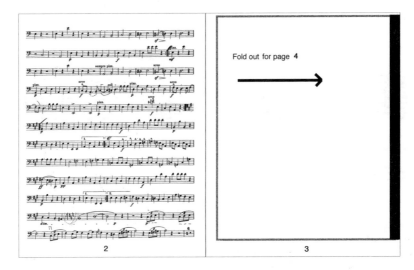

Example 3: Three page foldout

Tape the photocopied page to the left edge of the verso (the real page 4) so it will fold into the part and lay over the top of page 3. Trim the photocopied page to a width slightly less than the printed page so it folds easily inside the part. The player will then open the photocopied page out to the right in order to view all three pages. The player will then have to be instructed not to play the printed page 4, but to read from page 5 after turning the page. Cover the original page 4 with a blank sheet of paper, or use an adhesive "post-it" note to remind the player to continue on to page 5.

A four-page layout could also be created, if necessary. In Example 3, if there was no suitable place to turn at the bottom of page 1, a photocopy of that page could be taped to the left side of page 2. Tape the photocopy to the right side of the original page 1 (recto) so it folds to lay face down over the printed page 2 (verso). The player would then fold out both photocopies, laying page 1 to the left and page 4 to the right, creating a four-page spread.

These foldout pages create more work for the player, but depending on the printed layout of the music, there may be no other alternative. Remember that fold-out pages are better suited to a single player reading from one part. String players and others who play two to a stand and share a part must always read music at an angle, not directly on, as a single player would. While they may be comfortable with reading music from a two-page layout at a distance of two feet or more, an additional third page may be difficult to see.

- For players who share a single part, an alternative to the foldout page is to create a flap that folds in on the printed part. This way the photocopied music will lie inside the margins of the existing printed part.

In Example 4, there is not enough time to turn from page 3 (recto) to page 4 (verso) during the fermata. Also, an entire section of violas turning a page during a quiet fermata would disturb the performance. Because two players read from this viola part, a more convenient solution is to photocopy the first two staves of page 4 onto page 3 as a flap so the copied music is easily read within the boundaries of the printed part.

[page 3]
recto

[page 4]
verso

Example 4: Awkward turn between pages 3 and 4.

To create the flap, photocopy the first two staves of page 4, trim away unrelated information, and cut the photocopy to less than the width of the part. Paste the photocopy onto another piece of paper, which is cut slightly larger than the photocopy in order to leave a margin around each edge of the music. The background paper should be a different color than the part to help show a distinction between the printed music on the part and the photocopied music on the flap. Alternatively, using a wide tip felt marker, draw a border around the edge of the flap to make it stand out from the page it overlays. This will help the player easily discern the difference between the flap and the original part that lays underneath it (Example 5).

Example 5: First two staves of page 4 copied and laid onto a flap with a border.

The instruction "Turn page" at the bottom right corner of the flap will remind the player where to go next on the part.

Lay the flap so that it is face down over the bottom of page 3. Tape the left edge of the flap onto page 3 so that the loose edge opens to the left and lays across page 2. The flap should not extend past the edge of the printed part. On the back of the flap, add the note "Flip Flap" or "Open Flap" and a directional arrow to show which way the flap will open. Pick a location on page 3 that will allow the player time to flip the flap in advance and write an instruction to remind the player to open the flap ahead of time (Example 6).

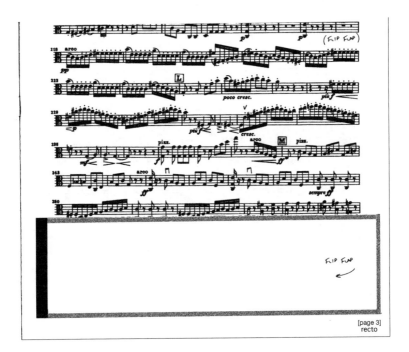

Example 6: Flap, taped in place, lays over page 3.

Now the musician can play all of page 2 and onto page 3. At the designated point, the musician will flip the flap to the left and continue playing to the end of page 3. Write the instruction "To Flap" after the last measure on page 3 to remind the player where the music continues. The musician will then play the passage copied onto the flap and the instruction "turn page" will direct them to turn the page and continue playing on page 4 (Example 7).

Example 7: Flap, opened to show the music copied from page 4.

On page 4, show the player where to begin again after the page turn. This example was marked with a post-it note to cover the music reproduced on the flap and an arrow indicating the next passage (Example 8).

Example 8: On page 4, the arrow indicates where to continue playing.

In extreme circumstances when there is no convenient way to accommodate page turns in a printed part, the part itself may need to be photocopied, cut, and pasted into a layout that allows time for proper page turns. Often it is only one or two pages that will need to be altered. These can then be taped or glued back into the original part. In extreme situations, the entire part will need to be recopied to fix the problem. Many liberties can be taken at this point, creating more or fewer pages than the original part and enlarging or reducing the size of the music itself to fit on the page, as long as the notes are still legible and easily read. In general, however, try to keep the physical size of the new part close to the original for ease in storing it with the set.

To set up better opportunities for turns, it is perfectly acceptable to leave a page blank or fill only part of the page with music (Example 9).

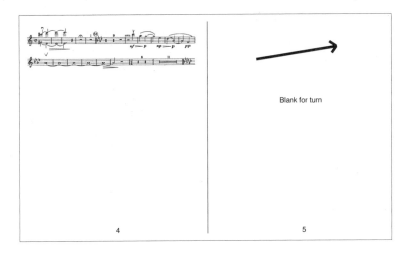

Example 9: Blank space used to accomodate a turn.

As you cut, copy, or tape over parts to fix bad page turns, watch closely to be sure you don't inadvertently cover up or omit information that the player will need, including clefs, meter signatures, dynamics, tempo indications, or musical instructions. When you are finished, count measure numbers or compare your repaired part against the score to be sure that all the notes and measures are still in place.

Many of the page turn fixes can be glued or taped in the margin of the existing part without altering the format of the original. Other corrections can be laid over the top of the existing music. If you are fixing a rental part or piece borrowed from another library, use removable tape to fix your turns, in case the owner wants the part restored to the original format.

Remember that all alterations should keep the part readable and easy to follow. Offer this library service to your musicians so that you know the music will be corrected properly and efficiently.

Making Copies

Photocopying music in the performance library is a necessary evil. While we must be respectful of the copyright law and not maliciously deprive any composer or publisher of their due, there are legitimate instances when the photocopier will act as a force for good. It is helpful, then, to know your copy machine well and understand what makes a good, useful photocopy.

As always before any photocopying project, clean the glass on your photocopier so that specks or dust will not show up on your new part.

1. Be sure the copied image (or page of music) fits completely on the page. No part of the image should be cut off or squeezed too close to the edge so as to be unreadable.
2. Center the image on the page. Leave a reasonable margin around all four edges—between ½ to 1 inch should be plenty. This margin will also allow room for the player to write performance notes.
3. Use as much of the page as possible. While this may seem a contradiction to the previous instruction, both concepts can work together. If you are copying an 8½ × 11 inch original onto a 10 × 13 inch piece of paper, enlarge the original so that it fills the larger paper and still leaves a reasonable margin. Placing the smaller image in the center of a larger piece of paper without enlarging it negates the purpose of using the larger page.
4. Keep the image straight on the page. Use the staff lines on the music to help you visually align the page so that the original is square on the glass before you run the copy.
5. Try to maintain the same top margin on each page. For example, when copying a score try to align the first staff the same distance from the top of the page on every copied page. If your original is inconsistent, do your best to fix this by adjusting the position of the original on the copier glass.
6. Think outside of the glass. If your original has a wide margin, slide the original off the copier glass so that only the image is reproduced and the margin is reduced. You can then enlarge the image slightly to fill up the extra space you have gained.
7. Light originals may be darkened to create better contrast between the notes and the paper. Experiment with your copier's exposure settings, trying photo as well as text settings to see which gives you the best contrast for that particular original.

Finally, be sure to check your finished product. If you are copying a score or part, open it and turn each page as if you were playing it. Make sure that each page is:

- In the correct order
- Not turned upside down
- Not skewed, distorted, or cut off

And remember to look for a double bar at the end of the piece so you know that you have copied all the pages from beginning to end.

Copying March Parts for Concert Use

For many years, marches for band were published on small paper stock, measuring approximately 7 inches wide by 5 inches tall. These were sized so they would fit easily on an instrument's music lyre for marching or outdoor performance.

Modern concert editions of marches are published in a larger format (9 × 12 inches or larger). This allows for better formatting and larger notes so the part is easier to read and play from. The larger parts are also easier to find in a player's music folder, whereas the smaller parts can be misplaced or damaged when mixed with the other larger music.

If you want to perform a march-size work on a concert program, a better solution is to photocopy the part and enlarge it so the music is easier to read and handle. Begin with the following steps:

- Gather one of each part from the set, selecting the best copy available. This will be the reproduction set. (See the article "Creating a Preservation Set.") Erase any extraneous markings from these parts that you don't want to appear on the newly copied set.
- As always before any photocopying project, clean the glass on your photocopier so that specks or dust will not show up on your new part.
- If available, use a heavier weight paper (60–70 lb. offset), which will be more durable and less opaque than typical office paper.
- Use standard-size paper, measuring 8½ × 11 inches.

There are two basic ways to enlarge the parts. Both are described below.

Vertical or "portrait" alignment

1. Choose a paper tray that feeds the short edge (8½ inch) of the paper through the machine first.
2. Set the enlargement feature on your photocopier to reproduce at 120% larger than the original.
3. Place one part on the copier glass so that the title of the part is face down and aligned with the short side of the glass.
4. You may need to adjust the part on the glass until the copy is centered on the page from left to right with enough room on top so that the title is easily readable.
5. If the music itself is cut off of the photocopy, or doesn't sufficiently fill up the page, adjust the enlargement percentage higher or lower to make the best use of the paper's width and height.
6. Copy as many parts as you need for your ensemble (2 each of the Flute part, 4 each of the Clarinet part, etc.).

The Juilliard School

M-85

Vertical or "Portrait" alignment

Horizontal or "landscape" alignment

1. Choose a paper tray that feeds the short edge (8½ inch) of the paper through the machine first.
2. Set the enlargement feature on your photocopier to reproduce at 154% larger than the original.
3. Place one part on the copier glass so that the title edge of the part is face down and aligned with the long side of the glass.
4. You may have to adjust the part on the glass until the copy is centered on the page from left to right with enough room on top so that the title is easily readable.
5. If the music itself is cut off of the photocopy, or doesn't sufficiently fill up the page, adjust the enlargement percentage higher or lower to make the best use of the paper's width and height.
6. Copy as many parts as you need for your ensemble (2 each of the Flute part, 4 each of the Clarinet part, etc.).

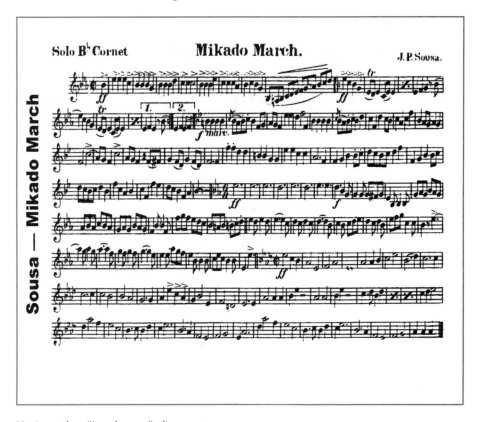

Horizontal or "Landscape" alignment

Other features to add

PROPERTY STAMPS AND CATALOG NUMBERS

If your reproduction set of parts doesn't already include your library's property stamp or catalog number, you can add them to all the new photocopied parts as you go. Note that this feature works better with the Vertical or Portrait alignment.

1. Stamp your library property stamp and/or catalog number onto the back of a post-it note (below the sticky area) and affix it to the glass, centered below the part. You could also use a blank piece of paper and tape it to the glass.
2. Make all your photocopies, leaving the post-it note in place, so that each photocopied part will have the same property and catalog information in the same location. See the vertical or "portrait" alignment example.

TITLE STRIPS

You can also add the march's composer and title so it appears in the same location on each photocopied part. This feature is most helpful for a horizontal-aligned part, so that the information is easily seen when the part is in a music folder.

1. Type or print a strip of paper with the title and/or composer of the work.
2. Tape it facedown onto the copier glass, flush with the left or right edge of the glass (depending on which edge is scanned first on your copier model).
3. Align the part against the title strip.
4. Make all your photocopies, leaving the title strip in place, so that each photocopied part will have the same information in the same location. You may have to reduce the enlargement percentage in order to fit the entire part on the page.

Music Preparation checklist

_____ 1. Discuss bowings with your string principals. If there are complex divisi passages, discuss these as well.

_____ 2. Consult with the conductor to get any performance markings (dynamics, articulations, phrasings) that should be added before rehearsals begin. Consult with the soloist about any cuts that must be added to the ensemble's parts and conductor's score. For points one and two, see the articles:

- *How to Mark Parts*
- *Music Notation Guidelines*

_____ 3. Ensure that the conductor's score and the ensemble's parts are the same edition. If the rehearsal figures differ in any way, are inadequate, or are nonexistent, take steps so they match. See the article:

- *Rehearsal Figures*

_____ 4. If time allows, correct any errata in the parts or score. Use proper music notation practices when correcting these errors. In some cases, you may be responsible for proofreading the music yourself and you may then create an errata list for that work to share with other librarians. See the articles:

- *Music Notation Guidelines*
- *Errata*

_____ 5. As you are marking bowings and making repairs, add any courtesy markings for the player's convenience. If you notice any bad page turns, fix them. See the articles:

- *How to Mark Parts—Performance Aids for the Player*
- *Binding Music for Performance*
- *Fixing Page Turns*

_____ 6. Occasionally, in the course of fixing page turns or making repairs, you will need to make photocopies of the music. This also applies if you are working with a composer or arranger who is not providing performance-ready sets of music, or if you need to enlarge small, march-size editions of band music. For suggestions on photocopy practices, see the articles:

- *Making Copies*
- *Copying March Parts for Concert Use*

_____ 7. If you receive new compositions or arrangements, either as a commissioned work or as part of a young composer's program, you must be aware of how and what to communicate to these composers. See the article:

- *What to Tell Student Composers*

CHAPTER

6

REHEARSAL AND PERFORMANCE

Booking Parts into Folders

t's a good rule of thumb to book your folders only when all sets for the entire program are prepared.

- Put empty folders in score order with wind, brass, and percussion on top.
- Set folders in a pile on your left.
- Set pile of any concert-specific announcement sheets (rehearsal order, program order, cuts, instrumentation, etc.) to the right of the folder pile.
- Make sure all performance-ready sets are complete and in score order with w/b/p on top.
- Line up sets in performance order from left to right and to the right of the concert-specific announcement sheets.

For a program with three works on it (overture, concerto, symphony), you should now be facing five separate piles in the following order from left to right:

1. Folders
2. Concert-specific announcement sheets
3. Overture (1st work on program)
4. Concerto (2nd work on program)
5. Symphony (3rd work on program)

- *It also may be helpful to have an ensemble roster handy on a clipboard. The clipboard ensures that the errant piece of paper won't accidentally be booked in a folder in the heat of assembly.*
- Assemble music and inserts for each folder by pulling from the top of each pile.
- Book into appropriate folder.

Pay close attention to which parts are going into which folder. As simple as this seems, one can get carried away with speed and put a bass clarinet part into a bassoon folder. Reducing your distractions during this process pays off.

- Place booked folder *face down* to the left of the empty folders.
- When all parts are in the folders, turn pile of booked folders right side up *et voilà*, folders are magically in score order.

You may also decide to establish a folder sign-out system. This can be as simple as having players initial by their name on the roster or as complex as scanning bar codes on the folder that corresponds to a database record belonging to the musician checking the part out. Whatever suits the needs of your organization is the best system for you.

Concert Duty Procedure

E very ensemble has its own routine for concert performances, determined as much by tradition as by necessity due to repertoire or the needs of the venue. Here are some general suggestions for the concert routine.

Before the concert

1. Arrive not later than one hour before the concert start time.

2. Put folders on the stands for the first work of the program.
   If there are any problems with the stage setup, notify the stage crew. Do not make changes to the stage setup yourself unless you are responsible for doing so. Some venues require that only their personnel are allowed to move equipment on the stage.

3. Keep any additional folders backstage in the music box/cart/trunk.[1]
   If there are folders that are not used for the first work, keep them nearby backstage and put them out as needed between selections during a change in the stage arrangement or seating. In some cases, folders for a later work can be placed behind another folder on a nearby music stand. If time is tight during a stage change, you could ask the players to move the folder to the appropriate location.

4. Collect concert programs for the performance library.

   - Three copies for the library files
   - Three copies for each rental piece on the program (Publishers typically request that two or three copies of the concert program be returned with the rental music for their royalty reports.)
   - Additional copies as needed for ASCAP/BMI reports, archival collection, etc.

5. At no later than five minutes before the concert begins, collect the scores from the conductor for the first half of the program.

6. Put only one score out at a time, unless the conductor requests otherwise or other arrangements have been made due to the flow of the program. Keep the other scores for the first half in the music cart.

7. Place the score in the center of the conductor's stand, opened to the first page of music, unless the conductor has other preferences.

---

1 Many librarians have an area backstage for additional folders, backup parts, and extra scores, sometimes even library supplies (tape, pencils, paper). Depending on the venue, it could be a portable music box, a library cart, or a tour trunk. The further away from your home library, the more convenient it is to have a safe and secure area for library materials.

8. If the conductor asks that their baton be put on the stand, place it horizontally on the stand with the handle facing to the right side so the conductor can pick it up easily.

9. During your time onstage, take a moment to look around and see if anyone or anything is out of place. Your ensemble's personnel manager and stage crew will take care of the players and the physical issues onstage. However, when carrying out the score you may be the last staff member on the stage, so use that time to check the stage once more before the performance begins.

10. Stay nearby backstage until the concert begins, in case of emergency. If possible, wait at least until the first note of music is heard.

Note that some libraries record the duration of the works on the program for performance records or for the conductor's personal information. If necessary, have a stopwatch ready backstage and pay close attention to the performance in order to document the total timing and/or the movement timings.

IN THE INTERVAL BETWEEN WORKS ON THE PROGRAM

11. Exchange the conductor's score, removing the old one and placing the new one in the center of the conductor's stand, opened to the first page of music.

12. Place any additional folders, remove any unnecessary folders, and/or move any previously set folders to their new location for the next work on the program, as time allows. Remember that you are also confirming any stage changes that affect the players and their music. Work with the stage crew to fix any last minute problems.

     Some typical stage changes involve:

     • Moving players to accommodate a soloist at the front of the stage
     • Reduction or enlargement in the number of players
     • Change in stage arrangement to accommodate the requirements of the work
     • Depending on the extent of the stage change, the librarian should remain nearby to ensure that the appropriate folders are on the correct stands before the players return to their seats

AT INTERMISSION

13. Add, remove, or move any folders, as necessary. Confirm the new stage setup.

14. At no later than five minutes before the concert continues, collect the scores from the conductor for the second half of the program.

AFTER THE CONCERT

15. Return the scores and batons to the conductor. If the conductor is too busy to take the scores from you backstage, put them in his/her dressing room or green room.

16. Collect the folders in score order, if possible, to be sure you have them all.

17. Before you leave, take one last walk around the back of the stage, checking the setup to make sure you didn't leave any folders on the stands.

This procedure works well for a seated ensemble using music folders. Some smaller ensembles (wind ensembles, chamber music ensembles, or contemporary music ensembles) have such a flexible instrumentation that each work necessitates a different seating arrangement. Using music folders for these ensembles would require shifting folders for each work and would simply slow down the stage changes.

In these situations, it may be better to let the players carry their own parts onstage and offstage after each work. The librarian could then stand by the stage entrance and collect the music from the players as they exit the stage.

What to take with you to the concert site

- At least one extra copy of each score (in case the conductor needs a score or in case a wind player forgets their part)
- All back stand string folders (in case a string player forgets their part)
- Emergency repair kit, containing:

  » Bowing pencils
  » Eraser
  » Six-inch ruler
  » Binding tape
  » Scotch tape (adhesive and removable, if available)
  » An assortment of colored pencils and markers
  » Large and small paper clips and binder clips
  » Loose sheets of white and colored paper
  » Pad of note paper (letter or legal size)
  » Metronome and/or tuner, with extra batteries

This may seem like a lot of supplies to carry, but they could all be stored in an envelope or stationery box to travel with the music cart. It is better to be prepared for emergencies such as:

- Last minute bowing changes or cuts that need to be marked (or erased)
- Parts that need to be repaired or rebound
- Messages that need to be posted backstage for the players
- Instructions from the conductor that must be written down and passed to the players
- Anything else that can possibly go wrong

Collecting Parts

The final chord has sounded and the rousing applause subsided. Audience members are departing the concert hall and musicians are packing up their instruments. Librarian to the stage.

There are two options when picking up folders:

1. Take the folders directly from the musicians' stands.
   Pros: More likely to get everything back
   Cons: If there is a quick stage change, you will be in the way of the stage crew

2. Ask musicians to drop off their folders in conveniently located boxes offstage.
   Pros: Works when there is no time to collect folders from the stage
   Cons: You may collect fewer folders if musicians forget to place them in the boxes

Whichever method you choose, you should alert your musicians early and often of how they should return their music, particularly if your ensemble performs sporadically. Remember, you will not be able to make an announcement immediately before the concert begins with the audience sitting in their seats and the maestra cooling her heels. An announcement at several times during the final or dress rehearsal should cover your bases. Not all of your musicians may be performing on all pieces, so make sure you've covered that contrabassoonist who only plays on the overture.

Ideally, you will have the time to collect folders from the stage. It's always nice to have the musicians close their folders with all their music inside and leave it on their stand. It makes pickup clean and quick, particularly if you pick the folders up in score order.

Don't forget to climb into the organ loft if there's an organ part or head to the wings to pickup the offstage parts. Also, make sure you've been able to collect any library-owned scores loaned to your conductor. You may not get another chance.

Breaking Down Folders

nce you're back in the library, follow the procedure below to dismantle your folders:

- Put the folders in score order
- Determine which folders are missing based on your roster
- Once all folders are present, turn the stack upside down. This means you will find the last instrument upside down and on top of the stack. This could be any percussion, keyboard, or auxiliary instrument, depending on the instrumentation of the concert.
- Reverse the process you completed when booking the folders
- As you empty a folder, lay out the sets in performance order from left to right, including a stack for any concert-specific announcement sheets

For a program with three works on it (overture, concerto, symphony), you should now be facing five separate piles in the following order from left to right:

1. Folders
2. Concert-specific announcement sheets
3. Overture (1st work on program)
4. Concerto (2nd work on program)
5. Symphony (3rd work on program)

This is when all that dutiful part-numbering really pays off. You can easily monitor your progress with those large and legible numbers at the top of each unique part.

- It also may be helpful to have an ensemble roster handy on a clipboard. This provides a quick way to identify who has any missing parts.
- When the folder is emptied, place it face up on the right side of all your sets.

Returning Rental Music

Most publishers ask that you erase your markings from the rental set before you return it. This is as much a courtesy to the next renter as it is to the publisher. Consider how you would like to receive the music and act accordingly. Do not erase certain markings which may be helpful to the next renter:

- String bowings
- Harp pedalings
- Note corrections or other errata that were found during the rehearsals
- Comments that may be helpful to the next player, such as "listen to flute"

Do erase:

- Unnecessary comments, phone numbers, messages between players, etc.
- Player notes such as "listen to Bob," since "Bob" may not be playing for the next ensemble
- Caricatures of the conductor, etc.

1. Gather all parts and scores together:

   a) Performance set
   b) Extra parts
   c) Rental scores on loan to conductors or players

2. Gather all paperwork associated and received with this rental.
3. Put the parts in the publisher's score order.
4. Compare the annotated inventory form (see the article "Receiving Music—Rentals") to the materials in hand. Make a note of any missing parts or other discrepancies.
5. If any parts are missing from the performance set, check the sign-out sheet and call or e-mail the player, telling them to return the music immediately.
6. When all the materials are together, find a sturdy box or envelope to accommodate all the parts and scores. (The box that was used to ship the music from the publisher may still be in the library.)
7. Include with the parts:

   a) The original copy of the publisher's packing slip or inventory
   b) Three copies of the concert program (as stipulated in the rental agreement)

   However, do not include your marked copy of the inventory, any invoices, billing statements, or contracts. Keep these for your records.

8. Arrange the music neatly in the box with the inventory and the programs on top. Fill the rest of the box with packing materials to reduce shifting during transport.
9. Close and tape the box securely.
10. Affix a mailing label to the package with the proper return address.[2]
11. Most publishers stipulate in their contract that the music be insured when it is returned to their office. Coordinate with your mail room or shipping agent to insure the package for a amount sufficient to replace the music if lost or no less than the rental fee.
12. Record the shipment in your shipping log and/or your acquisitions tracking database.

---

2   Some publishers supply their own return mailing labels. Others use an agent to store, ship, and receive their materials. Make sure the package is returned to the proper address.

Putting Away Concert Music

After breaking down the concert folders:

1. Check through the set and make sure all the parts are in order. The wind set should already be numbered and the string set should already have stand numbers to make this step easier.
2. Make a note of any parts that are missing or damaged beyond repair. Order replacement parts and, if possible, bill the player according to the library's policy.
3. Arrange the music in order (from top to bottom): wind set, strings, extra parts, scores (if stored with the set)
4. Record the event on the performance record and/or in the performance database. Make a note of any changes or adjustments to the music (cuts, retouches, etc.), especially those that are left in the parts so that you are reminded the next time this set is used.
5. Neatly arrange and straighten the stack of music, close the folder and put the music back on the shelf.

Rehearsal and Performance checklist

These steps cover getting the music out of the library to the players and getting it back again to where it belongs.

_____ 1. When all the parts are processed and ready to distribute to the players, put them in folders or on the music distribution shelf in preparation for the first rehearsal. See the article:

- *Booking Parts into Folders*

_____ 2. If you are required to work at concert performances, be aware of the special needs and protocols involved. See the article:

- *Concert Duty Procedure*

_____ 3. Following the performance, collect the folders or music parts from the players. See the article:

- *Collecting Parts*

_____ 4. Back in the library, remove the parts from the folders so they can be returned to their proper home. See the article:

- *Breaking Down Folders*

_____ 5. Rental music must be returned to the publisher promptly and in good condition. See the article:

- *Returning Rental Music*

_____ 6. For music in the library collection, document the event in the performance record and return the music to the shelves. See the article:

- *Putting Away Concert Music*

CHAPTER

7

ADDITIONAL
RESPONSIBILITIES

What to Tell Student Composers

Written as an open letter to a student composer

The readability of your printed music will determine, in part, the quality of the performance you receive. If your players can't easily interpret the printed page, they won't perform your music as well as it deserves. Remember also that first impressions are important—a clear and legible part will psychologically influence the player's attitude toward your music before they hear a note.

Even though most composers and copyists use a computer to create their performance materials, you should not expect the software to automatically spit out perfectly formatted parts. Examine each one for readability and formatting. Be familiar with proper music notation practice (see the bibliography at the end of this article for a list of recommended books). Know the ranges and transpositions of the instruments or consult an orchestration manual. If you write a passage or ask for a technique that you are not clear about, don't hesitate to ask a player, "Is this playable on your instrument," or "Is this the proper way to notate this passage." Most will be happy to offer their advice.

Consider these points before printing your instrumental parts

1. **Staff size and note head size.** This is an important factor in determining readability. Keep in mind that string players will be sharing a music stand, reading the notes from over two feet away and at a 45-degree angle. Consequently, a larger note size will be easier to read in these circumstances.

   Set your software to use a staff size no smaller than 85% (when using Finale) or .28 inches (when using Sibelius). The latter measurement refers to the distance between the bottom and top lines of the staff.

   You may also be able to reduce the margins of the pages to between .5 and .75 inches on each edge to allow more room for the larger staff size.

2. **Page turns.** You must allow adequate time for the player to turn pages. Plan for several measures of rest, if possible, at the end of a right hand page (the *recto*) or the beginning of a left hand page (the *verso*). It is acceptable to leave a page completely or partially blank if that helps set up good turns on the following pages.

   In extreme situations, you may be able to create a foldout page or an internal flap to help facilitate turns. Ask a librarian for assistance.[1]

---

1 For instructions on creating a foldout, flaps, and page turns, see the chapter on "Music Preparation." More details can be found in *A Manual for the Performance Library* by Russ Girsberger (Music Library Association Basic Manual Series, no. 6. Lanham, Md.: Scarecrow Press, 2006), 69–77.

3. **Rehearsal figures.** Measure numbers should appear on the left side of each staff. Do not number every measure, although it is helpful to add measure numbers before and after long multi-measure rests. For more instructions, see the article on "Rehearsal Figures."

4. **Include cues.** Your new music will not be familiar to the players. Include cues before important entrances or after long multi-measure rests. Choose a prominent line to cue, something that the player will hear easily within the texture of the piece from where they are sitting in the ensemble. Also make sure the cues are transposed to the key of the instrument reading the part.

5. **Label your parts clearly** (see Example 1). The first page of each part should have:

   • Title
   • Composer
   • Instrument name, with doublings indicated (ex.: 2nd Flute doubles on Piccolo)
   • Keys listed for all transposing instruments (clarinets, horns, and trumpets)
   • All percussion instruments needed by the player (see Example 2), with a notation key if the parts are complex

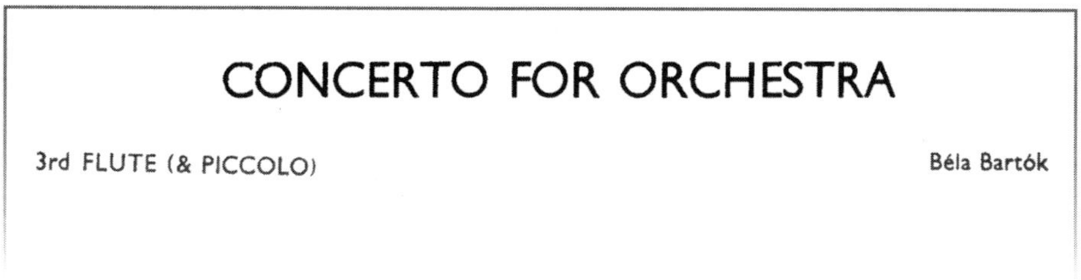

CONCERTO FOR ORCHESTRA

3rd FLUTE (& PICCOLO)   Béla Bartók

Example 1. Title page

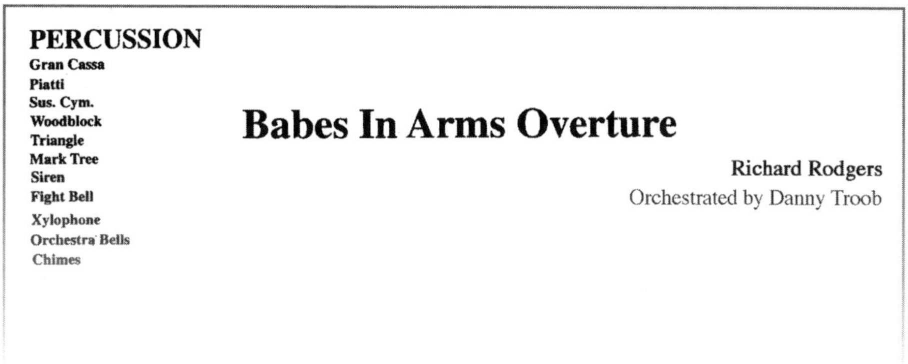

PERCUSSION
Gran Cassa
Piatti
Sus. Cym.
Woodblock   **Babes In Arms Overture**
Triangle
Mark Tree
Siren   **Richard Rodgers**
Fight Bell   Orchestrated by Danny Troob
Xylophone
Orchestra Bells
Chimes

Example 2. Percussion title page

All interior pages should have the instrument name and a page number. (see Example 3)

Example 3. Interior page

6. **Format your parts clearly.** As in any printed book, the pages on the right side (the recto) are odd numbered pages (1, 3, 5, 7, etc.), while the pages on the left side (the verso) are even numbered pages (2, 4, 6, 8, etc.).

If your music begins on the verso (page 2) of a part, in order to accommodate good page turns, create a cover sheet to serve as page 1 (See Example 4).

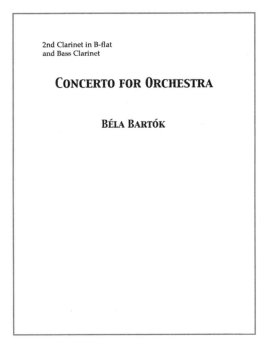

Example 4: Cover sheet

7. **Instrument changes and mute changes should be marked in two places:**

   a) Immediately after the last passage before the change
   b) Immediately before the affected passage

8. **Explain any non-standard notation or techniques.** Place these instructions at the beginning of the part or as a footnote on the same page as the action.

9. **Paper size.** Typical sizes of orchestral parts used by music publishers are 9 × 12 inches, 9½ × 12½ inches, or 10 × 13 inches. Parts measuring 11 × 14 inches are less common and anything larger is unwieldy for orchestral players.

10. **Paper weight.** Use paper of a sufficient weight and opacity so that the parts will stay upright on the music stand and notes and pencil markings on one side do not show through on the other.

    A common paper weight for parts and scores is 60 to 70 lb. offset. Light cream-colored paper will not reflect glare from stage lights and also allows for good contrast between the paper and the printed notes. Do not use paper labeled as "bright" white, which can cause eyestrain after extensive use.

11. **Binding.** Do not bind orchestra parts of less than 30 pages (15 sheets) with comb or coil binding. Use a tape binding system that allows the pages to lay flat and turn easily. See the article on "Binding Music" for more information.

Consider these points before printing your conductor scores

1. The score should be easily readable from a distance of two feet. The size of the staff and the printed note heads should be appropriate to the density of the orchestration and the notation.
2. The score should be no larger than 11 × 17 inches.
3. Use a spiral coil binding along the entire left edge of the score. If possible, do not use plastic comb bindings.
4. The cover should include the work title and the composer's name.
5. The first page should contain the complete instrumentation of the work (see Example 5), including:

    a) All instrument doublings (ex.: 2nd Flute doubles on Piccolo)
    b) Keys of the clarinets, horns, and trumpets
    c) All percussion instruments needed, with a notation key if the parts are complex
    d) An estimated duration of the total work and of individual movements, if applicable
    e) An explanation of any non-standard notation, staging, or instructions

6. The body of the score should include:

    a) Measure numbers on the left margin of each stave, large enough to be read at a distance of two feet
    b) Additional rehearsal figures (if used) should be letters or the appropriate measure number set in large type inside a circle or box

Concerto for Orchestra

by Béla Bartók

Duration: 36:00   movements: 1) 10:00; 2) 6:00; 3) 7:00; 4) 4:00; 5) 9:00

Instrumentation

3 Flutes   (3rd Flute doubles on Piccolo)

3 Oboes   (3rd Oboe doubles on English Horn)

3 Clarinets in B-flat   (3rd Clarinet doubles on Bass Clarinet)

3 Bassoons   (3rd Bassoon doubles on Contrabassoon)

4 Horns in F

3 Trumpets in C

3 Trombones

1 Tuba

1 Timpani

2 Percussion [Snare drum, bass drum, crash cymbals, suspended cymbal, tam-tam, triangle]

2 Harps

Strings

Example 5: Instrumentation sheet

Annotated bibliography

Del Mar, Norman. *Anatomy of the Orchestra*. Berkeley, Los Angeles: University of California Press, 1981.

> Del Mar describes the organization, arrangement, and performance practice of the modern symphony orchestra. Each section examines an instrumental family (strings, woodwinds, etc.) and outlines typical ranges, their appearance in the score, notation and layout of the parts, and typical or unusual effects. The many musical examples are taken from the orchestral literature.

Gerou, Tom, and Linda Lusk. *Essential Dictionary of Music Notation*. Los Angeles: Alfred Publishing, 1996.

> A pocket guide and ready reference manual, arranged in dictionary form, defining music notation terminology and illustrating standard notation practice.

Gould, Elaine. *Behind Bars: The Definitive Guide to Music Notation*. Harlow, England: Faber Music, 2011.

> Written by an editor at Faber Music, this rule manual for music notation includes over 1,500 musical examples, but also discusses page formatting and layout for parts and score.

Major Orchestra Librarians' Association. "Music Preparation Guidelines for Orchestral Music." Philadelphia, Pa.: Major Orchestra Librarians' Association, 2004.

> A pamphlet with guidelines for the proper formatting of orchestral music parts and scores, emphasizing readability and function. Available online at http://www.mola-inc.org/pdf/GuidelinesBrochure.pdf.

Powell, Steven. *Music Engraving Today: The Art and Practice of Digital Notesetting*. 2nd ed. New York: Brichtmark Music, 2007.

> A modern counterpart to the Ross manual (below), focusing on computer software programs such as Finale and Sibelius. It has invaluable information for every copyist and desktop music publisher.

Read, Gardner. *Music Notation: A Manual of Modern Practice*. 2nd ed. New York: Crescendo, 1969.

> Detailed explanations and examples of traditional notation, with chapters on instrumental, jazz, and vocal music. Part IV covers manuscript writing, proofreading, and preparing a score and parts.

Ross, Ted. *The Art of Music Engraving and Processing: A Complete Manual, Reference and Text Book on Preparing Music for Reproduction and Print*. 2nd ed. Miami, Fla.: Charles Hansen, 1970. CD-ROM publication: Santa Rosa, Calif.: npc Imaging, 2001.

> A comprehensive manual describing the historical process and practice of engraving music manuscript and the rules of notation applied to professional music printing.

Solomon, Samuel Z. *How to Write for Percussion: A Comprehensive Guide to Percussion Composition*. New York: SZSolomon, 2002 [www.szsolomon.com].

A detailed book on contemporary percussion composition and notation, it includes many musical examples, photos, and charts to illustrate contemporary performance practice and technique.

Stone, Kurt. *Music Notation in the Twentieth Century: A Practical Guidebook*. New York: W. W. Norton, 1980.

A textbook describing contemporary notation, written in two parts, covering: 1) general conventions of notation, pitch, duration, score and parts, rhythm, and indeterminate events, and 2) specific notation for instruments including keyboard reductions, voice, and taped sound.

What to Tell Student Conductors

Written as an open letter to a student conductor

Your school years are very busy as a student conductor. You are learning new repertoire, attending every rehearsal you can sneak into, and accepting every opportunity to conduct that comes your way. This is what school is for—a time to immerse yourself in music and grab every experience available.

It is also a prime opportunity to learn how to interact with other musicians and administrators. Take time to learn the function of each administrative department in your ensemble and how they work together to keep the organization operating smoothly. Sharpen your interpersonal skills so that you communicate efficiently and professionally. As a conductor leading an ensemble, these departments will be coming to you for information and decisions so they can do their jobs. Honing these abilities now will make you a good colleague in your future career.

Some fundamental personal characteristics are always appreciated by others, no matter what your profession.

Preparation

Plan ahead. As more people look to you for decisions, it is important to be prepared with ideas and answers. The activities of many other offices depend on the timely delivery of information, from repertoire choice to rehearsal schedules. Keep the organization moving forward by making sure the information flows efficiently.

Know your timetables and deadlines. Procrastination is never a virtue, especially if others are waiting on you. Each office has its own workflow and disrupting those schedules will make others work harder to catch up. Keep your professional calendar current so you are aware what to prepare and when it should be delivered.

Pick a plan and go with it. Music is an art, but it can also be a business. Don't change your concert repertoire just because you have realized a "better" programming idea. That will affect everyone—from the librarian to the personnel manager to the stage crew to the promotions department to the box office staff—and require them to work harder to accommodate the change. There are indeed times when a program will need to be changed on short notice: soloist cancellations, personnel changes, illness, death, or even significant current events. Everyone will understand these situations and pitch in to help because it is for a tangible cause and not just to accommodate an artistic whim.

Communication

Communicate early and often. It is never too soon to share information about an upcoming program. Each ensemble office operates on a tight schedule, juggling many projects simultaneously, and coordinating their activities with other departments.

Advance notice about repertoire and scheduling allows them to incorporate your project into their own workflow.

Each office requires some of the same information, which they will parse for their own use. The librarian needs to know the works you want to program so they can rent, purchase, and prepare the music. Other offices will assign players to the program, coordinate the rehearsal schedules, arrange for the necessary equipment and instruments, and prepare the rehearsal and performance site for the ensemble.

Looking at the individual responsibilities of each office, the logistics of coordinating all of these disparate elements to put on a performance seems almost insurmountable, but efficient communication at all levels helps each process to move smoothly. And the first step in many of these processes starts with you, the conductor.

What the librarian can do for you

Even as a student, you shouldn't hesitate to ask for information or advice from your performance librarian. When it comes to the music itself, the librarian can assist you in a number of ways, both as you are considering repertoire for your programs and after you have chosen it.

Repertoire research. The librarian has access to a wide variety of resources: reference books, publisher catalogs (both print and online), music dealers, and library colleagues in other ensembles.

If you wish to program a work you are unfamiliar with, your librarian can help locate it and possibly secure a perusal score or recording for your study. Provide as many details as you can about the work, including the publisher (if known) and where you heard about the work (recording, live performance, radio broadcast). The more information you can provide about the piece, the easier it will be to track it down.

Librarians can also advise you on the relative merits of editions and publishers to help choose from the available options. Depending on the composer or composition, this can lead to many questions that need to be answered first before the music is ordered. Some examples of basic concerns include:

- If you program a Mozart symphony, which published edition should you use?
- If you have chosen a Bruckner symphony, which incarnation of the work do you want to hear?
- If you plan to conduct from a Dover score, are the rehearsal figures compatible with those in the instrumental parts?

Marking bowings and edits. If you have specific bowings to use for your performance, get them to the librarian in a timely manner so they can put them into the parts for you. The same goes for cuts, inserts, and other musical markings (dynamics, articulations, and phrasing). Marking this information in advance will save a great deal of rehearsal time. Note these caveats, however:

- Depending on the situation, some information is more efficient to share through a brief announcement from the podium or with the appropriate baton gesture.

- The more "dots and dashes" you include, the longer it will take for the library staff to prepare the parts. Give this information to the librarians well in advance of the event so there is plenty of time to schedule it as part of the library workflow.
- If you are appearing as a guest conductor with an orchestra that has an established sound and performance style, beware of asking too much or of imposing an unorthodox interpretation upon your hosts. If your markings are significantly different from the common practice, such as for a historical performance interpretation, consider purchasing and marking your own set of parts to use with your host orchestras. This is one way to ensure that the information is conveyed directly to the players and that your rehearsal time is used most efficiently.

What you can do for your librarian

Share information early. The issues may be large (changing repertoire on short notice) or small (adding an assistant player to the horn section), but the sooner the librarian knows, the easier it is to address the issue and incorporate it into their workflow.

Educate yourself on the relative merits of editions. Your librarian can help with this issue by advising you on what editions are available and the positive and negative features of each, at least from the librarian's or performer's point of view. They can also ask their colleagues what edition of a work is being used by other orchestras.

Keep in mind that the latest "critical edition" on the market may not be the best choice to use as a performing edition. Such a decision should also take into consideration the following issue.

Look at the parts. The view from the players' stands is different from the view from behind the score, sometimes significantly so. Occasionally works that have an engraved full score have instrumental parts reproduced from hand manuscript. Poor page layout and awkward page turns can also hinder a player's performance and printed mistakes in the parts or score may raise questions in rehearsal. Some of these issues can and will be addressed by the librarian, depending on the amount of time and resources they have available. Know what materials the players are working with so you will understand these situations when they arise in rehearsal. For an example of some points to consider, read the article by Richard Payne in the bibliography below.

Discuss rehearsal figures. One of the first questions a librarian should ask after receiving a concert program is, "What score will you be conducting from, Maestro?" They ask this to ensure that the information in your score will match the information in the library parts, and the biggest issue is rehearsal figures. If your score has measure numbers, but the parts only have letters, you will waste a lot of rehearsal time trying to find common ground. The librarian can usually reconcile this issue before rehearsals begin, so be sure to share this information when you discuss editions.

Remember that all the participants (the players and all the administrative staff) want to work together to give the best possible performance, just as you do. If everyone works in concert, both on the stage and off, the organization can indeed make beautiful music together.

Annotated bibliography

Bloom, Peter, editor. *The Cambridge Companion to Berlioz*. Cambridge, New York: Cambridge University Press, 2000.

This is an example of the many series of composer studies and bio-bibliographies that are helpful in repertoire and historical study. Of particular interest in this volume is the chapter "Performing Berlioz," by D. Kern Holoman (pp. 173–196), and his discussion of the published editions of Berlioz. Note the three examples of published viola parts and how the system of rehearsal figures differs between them.

Bowen, José Antonio, editor. *The Cambridge Companion to Conducting*. Cambridge, New York: Cambridge University Press, 2003.

This collection of essays addresses several aspects of conducting, including working with choral music, early music, and opera repertoire, as well as providing an interesting perspective from the players point of view in the chapter, "The Orchestra Speaks" (pp. 79–90).

Burlingame, Marshall. "Staging an orchestra concert." *MadAminA* [Music Associates of America] 4, no. 1 (Spring 1983): 13–15.

A look at the many behind-the-scenes activities involved in preparing a performance, from the perspectives of the librarian, personnel manager, and music director. Available online at http://musicassociatesofamerica.com/madamina/1983/staging.html.

Daniels, David. *Orchestral Music: A Handbook*. 4th ed. Lanham, Md.: Scarecrow Press, 2005.

An invaluable guide to the standard orchestral repertoire, it contains instrumentation, duration, publisher addresses, and helpful programming information. The appendices categorize the works by duration, instrumentation, and nationality. An online version is available by subscription at http://www.orchestralmusic.com.

Del Mar, Norman. *Anatomy of the Orchestra*. Rev. ed. Berkeley: University of California Press, 1983.

This book describes the instruments and their individual and ensemble functions within the orchestra, with notes on performance practice, notation, and terms found in the repertoire.

Del Mar, Norman. *Orchestral Variations: Confusion and Error in the Orchestral Repertoire*. London: Eulenburg, 1981. Reprint, New York: Da Capo, 1982.

Del Mar identifies discrepancies in editions of forty-five works by twenty-two composers, raising many questions for consideration, but not always providing definitive answers. Although the book is somewhat dated, it still demonstrates the importance of studying and comparing editions.

Green, Elizabeth A. H. *The Dynamic Orchestra: Principals of Orchestral Performance for Instrumentalists, Conductors, and Audiences.* Englewood Cliffs, N.J.: Prentice-Hall, 1987.

With the help of several professional musicians, Green examines the musical, social, and professional functions of the orchestra, and includes chapters on orchestra protocol and bowing principles.

Lawson, Colin, editor. *The Cambridge Companion to the Orchestra.* Cambridge, New York: Cambridge University Press, 2003.

This volume in the Cambridge Companion series looks at aspects of the orchestra with a broad view of the ensemble's activities.

Leinsdorf, Erich. *The Composer's Advocate: A Radical Orthodoxy for Musicians.* New Haven: Yale University Press, 1981.

The renown conductor expresses his opinion on interpretation and adherence to the composer's vision, but also includes his views on the function and "tasks" of the conductor.

Martin, Nicholas Ivor. *The Da Capo Opera Manual.* New York: Da Capo Press, 1997.

One of the best reference sources on opera repertoire, Martin includes many production details, including act timings, choral requirements and solo roles, instrumentation, and publisher and rights information.

Payne, Richard. "Angels with dirty faces? Looking at the new, critical edition of Beethoven symphonies from Breitkopf & Härtel." *Broken Pencil* [Newsletter of the United Kingdom orchestra librarians] Issue no. 5 (Autumn 2004): 1–2.

The librarian of the London Philharmonic Orchestra surveys these new editions of standard repertoire works with an eye toward print quality, size, layout, page turns, and readability from the player's point of view. Available online at http://www.mola-inc.org/Broken_Pencil/BrokenPencil5-Autumn2004.pdf.

Spitzer, John, and Neal Zaslaw. *The Birth of the Orchestra: History of an Institution, 1650–1815.* Oxford, New York: Oxford University Press, 2004.

A well-documented history of the development of the orchestral ensemble and of orchestral music. The authors discuss chronological and nationalistic development, with separate chapters on seating and acoustics, performance practice, and orchestration. It is invaluable for the study of the orchestral repertoire in its historical context.

Sutherland, Robert, and Clinton F. Nieweg. "Editions Paper: A discussion of various editorial trends and how a conductor's decision to use a particular edition may impact the librarian." n.p.: Major Orchestra Librarians' Association, 1999.

A monograph addressing the relative benefits and drawbacks of various editions, including the current trend toward use of "critical editions" as performance material. Available online at http://www.mola-inc.org/PressRoom/EditionspaperJuly1999.pdf.

Preparing Audition Lists

Your orchestra is holding auditions to fill a vacancy. As librarian, you must consult with the personnel manager and the members of the audition committee to find out what music they want to hear. The librarian can also give advice on describing the works on the audition repertoire list, on editions, on the availability of music, and on securing permission if copyrighted music will be used. The librarian will also probably be responsible for preparing the excerpts for use by the auditionees and the audition committee.

As you compile the repertoire list of music to be heard, in effect telling the auditionees what they will be practicing for the next several weeks, it is important to be clear and accurate so that all involved know what to prepare on one side of the screen and what they can expect to hear on the other.

When selecting music for audition lists, there are four issues to consider: titles, editions, publishers, and access.

Titles

Be as specific as possible when identifying musical works. In particular, watch out for:

- Unfamiliar translated titles. *Die diebische Elster*, printed on some parts, is more commonly known as *The Thieving Magpie* or *La Gazza Ladra*.
- Works known by two titles. Richard Strauss's *Le Bourgeois Gentilhomme* is also known as *Der Bürger als Edelmann*.

Editions

The same work may be available in different states—either reworked by different arrangers, in different versions by the same composer, or published by several companies and annotated by different editors.

- The same work by different arrangers. Edwin F. Kalmus sells two suites of music from Strauss's *Der Rosenkavalier*, one arranged by Mandell and one by Nambuat. These differ from the suites arranged by Dorati, Leinsdorf, and Steinberg, although the version published by Boosey & Hawkes and arranged (most likely) by Rodzinski may be the most familiar version. Similar situations are seen with the many orchestrations of *Pictures at an Exhibition* and *Night on Bald Mountain*.
- Different versions of the work by the same composer. Some composers revised their music during their lifetime. For example, Stravinsky's *Petrouchka* is published in the original 1911 version and in a revised 1947 version. Mendelssohn's Fourth Symphony also exists in two published editions, the original and an 1834 revision. And Bruckner symphonies are notorious for the diversity of their various states. If an audition excerpt differs in any way between the

various states of a work, be sure to specify which one the audition committee wants to hear.

- The same work issued by different publishers. The differences between published editions may simply boil down to articulation markings, phrasings, bowings, or other details, rather than large structural changes. However, if these issues are important to the audition committee, be sure to identify the exact edition or publisher so there is no question about what the musicians are expected to play. If an auditionee plays a passage staccato rather than marcato, the committee should be sure that this is an issue of interpretation and not of different editorial markings on either side of the audition screen.

Publishers

Another, more significant point to consider about different published editions is how to identify the specific excerpt to be played. If one publisher uses rehearsal numbers while another uses rehearsal letters, it may be difficult for a player to find the correct passage to prepare.

For example, on a recent audition list, one orchestra asked for an excerpt from the overture to Rossini's *La Gazza Ladra*. A part published by Luck's Music Library had rehearsal letters, while a part published by Edwin F. Kalmus & Co. used the same rehearsal letters, but also added measure numbers. The miniature score published by Eulenburg has both measure numbers and rehearsal numbers, as does the miniature score published by Fondazione Rossini, but the two rehearsal number systems don't match. In this example, the orchestra's audition list identified the excerpt using the rehearsal numbers from the Eulenburg score, but this information was not communicated to the auditionees. This resulted in confusion for the players as well as several calls to the orchestra's personnel office to clarify this issue.

In another instance, an audition list identified a violin excerpt from Prokofiev's "Classical" Symphony using the rehearsal numbers found in the Edition Symphonique parts (reprinted by Broude Bros.). Unfortunately, some auditionees owned parts from the Editions Russe version (reprinted by Kalmus) which used rehearsal letters, and were unaware of the other edition.

In a more common situation, an audition list asked for an excerpt from Schubert's Symphony No. 9, with no additional identification provided. The numbering of the late Schubert symphonies can be inconsistent, to say the least. One reprint edition of a Breitkopf & Härtel publication is printed as "Symphony No. 7 in C Major" and is, in fact, the "Great" C major symphony, identified in Otto Erich Deutsch's catalog of Schubert's works as number D. 944. A later Breitkopf & Härtel edition (Nr. 4467) identifies the same work as "Symphonie Nr. 8," but helpfully includes the Deutsch catalog number on the part, while another Breitkopf & Härtel edition (Nr. 4468) identifies Schubert's "Unfinished" symphony (D. 759) also as "Sinfonie Nr. 8." The newest Bärenreiter edition of the "Great" C major symphony wisely avoids ordinal numbers entirely and simply identifies the work with the Deutsch catalog number, the key, and the subtitle.

Access

To hold a fair audition, every participant should have equal access to all music on the list. Tone, technique, and interpretation are all individual characteristics that will determine which player wins the audition, but each candidate should be playing, figuratively and literally, from the same page of music.

The ICSOM (International Conference of Symphony and Opera Musicians) Code of Ethical Audition Practices states, "All applicants should be sent...the complete audition repertoire (excluding sight-reading repertoire), and parts for announced excerpts not generally available." This document is available online at http://www.icsom.org/handbook/handbook13d.html.

Some music is available for sale to all. The reprint publishers Edwin F. Kalmus, Luck's Music Library, Broude Brothers Limited, and Subito Music Corporation all sell individual parts of the music in their catalogs. The Orchestra Musicians CD-ROM Library also sells instrumental parts to many public domain works, and many students get parts online from the International Music Score Library Project (IMSLP). See the article "Other Sources for Acquiring Music" for more suggestions of where to locate parts.

Music that is not available for purchase should not be included on an audition list unless arrangements have been made to provide it to all auditionees. Many contemporary works, still under copyright protection, may be acquired only through that publisher's rental department. This music is not available for sale or loan to individuals. Including these titles may put some auditionees at an unfair advantage if they don't otherwise have access to the music.

The organization holding the audition should arrange for these excerpts to be made available to all auditionees. This can be done through direct mailing to those auditionees who request it, or by posting the excerpts on a password-protected Internet website. If a work is still under copyright protection, contact the music publisher's rental library or their permissions department. Ask for permission to reproduce their music for use at an audition. Provide specific details, including the composer, title, instrument, and exactly what excerpt from the work will be used. Most publishers are willing to accommodate these requests. Some may ask for a small royalty payment while others may request that the copyright statement be printed on the music. Not securing permission for the use or reproduction of copyrighted music is a violation of the copyright law and may result in fines or criminal prosecution.

Another option is to locate the excerpt in a commercially published excerpt book and provide this information to the auditionees so they can acquire the book on their own. This, again, guarantees that all participants have equal access to the same music.

Some orchestras include additional details on their audition lists that clarify information or provide assistance to the auditionees. This can include item numbers from publisher catalogs, contact information where this music can be ordered, and the title and publisher of excerpt books that contain the excerpt.

MINNESOTA ORCHESTRA
Osmo Vänskä, Music Director

AUDITION REPERTOIRE
SECTION VIOLA

Auditions: May 13-17, 2004

SOLO REPERTOIRE

First movement of one of the following concerti (no accompaniment):

BARTOK	Viola Concerto
HINDEMITH	*Der Schwanendreher*
WALTON	Viola Concerto

One movement from any of the unaccompanied suites by Bach

ORCHESTRAL REPERTOIRE

1. BEETHOVEN — Symphony No. 5, second movement

2. BERLIOZ — *Roman Carnival* Overture

3. BRAHMS — Variations on a Theme by Haydn, Nos. 5, 7, 8

4. BRUCKNER — Symphony No. 4, second movement

*5. COPLAND — *Appalachian Spring*, Full Orchestra Version, rehearsal [6] to one measure before rehearsal [14]

6. MENDELSSOHN — Scherzo from *A Midsummer Night's Dream*

7. MOZART — Symphony No. 35, last movement

8. RAVEL — *Daphnis and Chloé*: Suite No. 2, rehearsal [158] to rehearsal [161]; three measures after rehearsal [212] to End

*9. SHOSTAKOVICH — Symphony No. 5, first movement: rehearsal [15] to rehearsal [17]

10. SIBELIUS — Symphony No. 3, first movement: rehearsal [6] to rehearsal [13] (♩ = 116-120)

11. STRAUSS — *Don Juan*, Beginning to rehearsal [E]

Most of the music for this audition is available from Kalmus publishers (contact information listed below). Those pieces noted with an asterisk (*) are rental only and may be requested from the Minnesota Orchestra Personnel Office using the enclosed form, which must be accompanied by a completed application and audition deposit.
NO EXCERPTS WILL BE MAILED WITHOUT RECEIPT OF ALL REQUIRED REGISTRATION MATERIALS.

Edwin F. Kalmus & Co., Inc.
P.O. Box 5011
Boca Raton, FL 33431
Phone: (561) 241-6340 – OR – (800) 434-6340 (outside Florida)
Fax: (561) 241-6347
www.kalmus-music.com

PLEASE NOTE: Screens will be used for all preliminary and semi-final rounds.

Audition list example. *Reproduced by permission of the Minnesota Orchestra.*

Preparing Digital Audition Excerpts

1. Determine the specific excerpt to be used, with clear start and stop points.

2. Clean the excerpt on the original part, erasing all unnecessary markings and filling in any faded lines or broken notes. If it is a string instrument part, make sure all bowings and other markings are legible. Confirm with the audition committee that bowings are to be included and that those included are approved.

3. Scan directly from the original part at full size. Save the file as either a black and white or greyscale TIFF or PDF file. The resolution should be between 300 to 600 dpi.[2]

4. In addition to the excerpt passage, copy additional passages that include the information below. Examine the music before the excerpt begins to determine which ones apply to the passage you need:

   - Clef sign
   - Key signature
   - Meter signature
   - Tempo markings and/or musical instructions
   - Key of the instrument, if the excerpt is for a transposing instrument (clarinet, horn, trumpet)
   - Any other applicable markings: mutes, playing instructions (sul pont., pizz., stopped horn)

   You may also want to scan the title page of the part along with the instrument name and composer's name to use as a header for the excerpt. Alternatively, you may enter all of this information on your computer using a standardized typeface and font size so that all excerpt information looks uniform.

   If you are preparing an excerpt from a copyrighted work, be sure to include any copyright information or permissions statement that the publisher requires as a condition for use of the work.

5. Open the image file in a software program such as Adobe Photoshop, Adobe Photoshop Elements, Corel Paint Shop Pro, or other applications that allow

---

2   The abbreviation dpi means dots per inch and is a measurement of the image resolution. Higher dpi (600) gives a better-looking image, but the size of the scanned file is larger. Lower dpi (150) yields a smaller file size, but the image is of lower resolution and lesser quality.

you to cut and paste segments of the image and manipulate them on the computer screen.

6. If your excerpt does not start at the beginning of the work or movement, copy and paste musical elements from before the excerpt begins to create a starting point with the appropriate information, which should appear in this order:

   - Clef sign
   - Key signature
   - Meter signature
   - Tempo markings and/or musical instructions (allegro, andante, etc.). Include metronome markings, if available
   - Any other applicable information: mutes, playing instructions (sul pont., pizz., stopped horn, etc.)

7. If the excerpt needs further cleaning or clarifying, do so using the software's erasing or drawing features.

8. When the excerpt is complete with start and stop points clearly identified, either erase all other markings that surround the excerpt, crop all extraneous images, or cut and paste the excerpt to a new, clean page.

9. Create a title header that includes the following information:

   - Composition title
   - Composer
   - Instrument. If the excerpt is for a transposing instrument (clarinet, horn, trumpet), be sure to include the key of the instrument
   - Any other information that pertains to the excerpt or this audition: no repeats, play second ending, etc.

   Enter this information on the image using the software's typesetting feature, or scan, copy, and paste it from the original part.

10. Adjust the image size so that it prints to standard letter size paper.

11. The final document should be saved or exported as a PDF (Portable Document Format) file so it will dislay on the screen the same to all readers, regardless of computer or software used. Be sure to embed all necessary fonts into your PDF file.

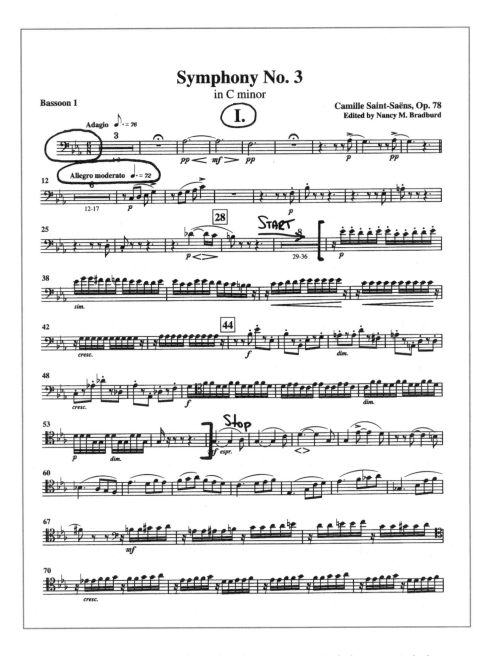

Full page with start and stop indicated and necessary musical elements circled.

Final excerpt with musical elements in place, image cropped, and identifying header.

Errata

E rrata (the plural of *erratum*) are mistakes in printed text, usually caused by an oversight in the editorial process or an error in the printing process. In book publishing they can cause the reader to reread a word or phrase to determine the intended meaning. In music publishing, these errors can cause the composer's intent to be misinterpreted and performed incorrectly, sometimes for many years, until scholarship or detective work discover the true intent.

It is important to be aware of errata. With all of the notes, stems, dots, and dashes in any piece of music, it is almost certain that there is a mistake somewhere, and there are works and editions that are more likely to have errors than others.

Consequently, the responsibility for correcting errata often falls to the performance librarian. It can be a time-consuming task, but this work will yield a more accurate performance and provide your musicians with a better product.

Documenting errata

In addition to correcting errata, the librarian should also be ready to take note of mistakes that they discover in the course of their work. The essay that follows, "Suggestions for Completing Errata Forms," was prepared by the Errata Committee of the Major Orchestra Librarians' Association in an effort to standardize the recording of errata information. The two documents at the end of the article are the current recommended forms for recording and sharing errata information. They may be reproduced for your own use.

Keep a blank copy of these documents handy with your other library master forms. If a player or conductor reports an error or if you notice one when you are marking parts, jot it down on an errata form and store it with your set. This will help you document changes made to your parts in case someone questions a decision and gives you a medium to share your findings with your colleagues.

Where to find errata information

The best way to find errata is to sit with the conductor's score and the set of parts, comparing one against the other. The goal for your rehearsals is to have the conductor's score match the player's parts so that no time is wasted in rehearsal with questions about the musical text.

This comparison may not answer all of the questions that arise in rehearsal, so it may also be helpful to have access to other sources:

- Earlier printings
- Piano reductions
- Same work issued by other publishers
- Score in the composer's collected works
- Facsimile reproductions

- Composer's manuscript
- Printed documents, such as correspondence between the composer and the publisher

This kind of in-depth research is undertaken when creating a critical edition of a work and these resources many not be available to most performance librarians. Other options are more readily available, however:

- Examine another set of parts that has already been used for rehearsal or performance and look for corrections written in by the players. If you don't have another set in your library, you may be able to borrow one from another ensemble, or at least visit their library and examine their parts on site.
- If the piece has been published in the composer's collected works edition, read the editor's comments. Some editions publish a companion "critical report" that documents all of the discrepancies found when examining the sources.
- Determine if there is an existing errata list. MOLA members have been creating and sharing errata lists for many years. If you are not a member, contact a librarian who is and ask if there is a list for the piece you are working on. The community of performance librarians has long been willing to share this information, applying the adage that many hands make light work. Correcting your set of parts from an existing errata list speeds your work and makes you more efficient.
- Contact other librarians or conductors. If you can't speak to your colleagues personally, visit an online group or chat room to ask if others know information that will help you. Some of these resources include:

  » Orchestra Library Information (OLI) Yahoo! Group, an online forum moderated by Clinton F. Nieweg, Principal Librarian (ret.) with The Philadelphia Orchestra. Members share information about repertoire, editions, and errata. Available online at: http://launch.groups.yahoo.com/group/OrchLibInfo/?yguid=137775693.
  » The Conductor's Guild sponsors their internet mailing list, "GuildList," available to members of the organization. Information is available at http://www.conductorsguild.org.
  » Listservs or message services sponsored by organizations or individuals, such as Orchestralist (http://www.orchestralist.net/olist/index.php), College Band Director's National Association (CBDNA) (http://www.cbdna.org), American Choral Directors Association ChoralNet (http://www.choralnet.org).

Errata information is occasionally published in journals or books. The bibliography below lists some of these resources.

The American Choral Review and *Research Memorandum Series*.

Each journal published quarterly. These publications of the American Choral Foundation are intended for the professional choral director or performer. The

Research Memorandum Series (RMS) occasionally publishes articles on musical editions and errata. Indexes to both journals are available online at http://www.chorusamerica.org. Back issues are available online to members only.

BD Guide.

Since its inception as *Band* magazine in 1984, this journal regularly included articles analyzing band and wind ensemble music. Many of these articles included errata lists, such the series by Frederick Fennell. The journal is no longer published, but some of these articles are reprinted in collections from Meredith Music Publications.

The Choral Journal.

Published ten times a year. This journal of the American Choral Directors Association (ACDA) occasionally includes articles on publishers, library collections, and errata. Online access is available through the ACDA website at http://acdaonline.org/cj/interactive.

Del Mar, Norman. *Orchestral Variations: Confusion and Error in the Orchestral Repertoire.* London: Eulenburg, 1981. Reprint, New York: Da Capo, 1982.

Del Mar identifies discrepancies in editions of forty-five works by twenty-two composers, raising many issues for consideration, but not always answering them. This collection expands on his articles originally published in *Score* magazine.

The Instrumentalist.

Published monthly. Intended for the instrumental music teacher, this magazine occasionally publishes analyses of band or wind ensemble works, some of which include errata. Several are reprinted in *The Instrumentalist Anthology Series* of books.

Journal of Band Research.

Published twice a year. This journal of the American Bandmasters Association features scholarly articles on bands, wind music, and related topics. Errata may be included in articles on analysis or performing editions.

Journal of the Conductors' Guild.

Published twice a year. Errata for orchestral, choral, and wind works are often published in this journal under the column "Scores and Parts." An online index to the journal is available through the Guild's website at http://www.conductorsguild.org. Access to back issues is available to members only.

Marcato.

Published quarterly. The newsletter of the Major Orchestra Librarians' Association (MOLA). Current and back issues are available online at http://www.mola-inc.org/marcato.html. Some issues include titles of works with available errata lists on file in the MOLA Resource Center. These lists are available to MOLA members through the organization's website.

Topolewski, Tim. "Errata Studies for the Wind Band Conductor." N.p.: various publishers, 1990–2000.

A five-volume set of monographs with incomplete errata for over thirty works in the
standard wind band repertoire. The individual booklets are available for purchase
from most music dealers and are advertised at http://www2.potsdam.edu/topolet/
errata.html.

Suggestions for Completing Errata Forms[3]

The new (2010) version of the MOLA Errata Form asks for more information than previous versions. We realize that not everyone will complete each field. However, we do ask that as much information as possible be provided if it is known and if time allows.

Status codes

! = Critical correction. Some users of errata lists do not have time to make every correction listed. In order to help our colleagues save time, please identify the most important corrections.

? = Requires a determination by librarian or conductor. In order to maintain consistency, the score matching the set of parts must be considered the primary reference. Any change from this point of reference must be documented when creating errata lists. When the score appears to be in error, corrections may involve the use of multiple references, performance practice, common sense, and/or opinion. Please list your reason for the change or document your other source(s).

A blank cell indicates that this correction is not critical and/or does not require determination.

The two basic purposes of status codes are to prioritize corrections and to document corrections that are not supported by the matching score. We suggest using the symbols "!" and "?" to flag corrections that are considered "critical corrections" or "require a determination" respectively.

- **What is a "critical correction?"** Any correction that has the potential to stop a rehearsal. Wrong pitches, rhythms, and missing bars tend to be critical. Wrong or missing dynamics, articulations, and tempo indications in solo or exposed lines may be considered critical. Although some types of corrections appear to be more important than others, please keep an open mind and exercise common sense when deciding. Staccato marks are almost never considered critical, but if a missing staccato dot means the difference between a slur and a hooked bowing, it has potential to stop a rehearsal and waste time.

---

3   This section is reprinted from the MOLA errata instructions. Used courtesy of the Major Orchestra Librarians' Association.

- **What type of correction "requires a determination?"** Any correction to a part that involves a deviation from the matching score. Although the score contains errors, just like the parts, it is important to use a "**?**" when a correction is not supported by the matching score. What appears to be a simple score error to one person may be a complex editorial decision to another. Please be diligent about using the "**?**" to identify all corrections not supported by the matching score, as this will allow the user to correct his parts without confirming each correction.

Instrument names

- Use standard instrument names or abbreviations to avoid confusion.
- The instrument name need be listed only once at the start of the corrections and at the start of each new page.

Referencing a specific place in the music

- **Movement:** If a work has multiple movements, use a Roman numeral to indicate the movement in the appropriate column.
- **Measure Numbers:** If a work has printed measure numbers, refer exclusively to measure numbers in the appropriate column.
- **Rehearsal Figures:** If a work has printed rehearsal figures, list the figure as well as the measure number before or after the figure in the respective columns. For example, **C**-3 refers to the third bar before rehearsal figure **C**.
- **No Rehearsal System.** If a work has no rehearsal system, it is advisable to add measure numbers, as this will be most universal. Please include in your notes a guide to the bar count and how you chose to handle difficult areas such as repeats and partial bars.
- **Beat:** Unless otherwise indicated, the beat refers to the denominator of the time signature, not necessarily to the pulse. For example, in 6/8 time, the beat is the eighth note, regardless of the tempo or pulse, and beat four will be the fourth eighth note of the measure.

Notating corrections

- If a notation is wrong, list the current indication followed by s/r (should read) and the correct indication.
- If an indication is in the wrong place, first reference the current position and then list the correct position.
- Be as clear as possible when listing corrections. Do not assume that someone making the corrections will be referring to the score.
- Typed errata lists are more readable and more easily transferred, but a handwritten list is better than none at all.

Suggestions

- If there are errors in the score, please create a list of score corrections and group them preceding the part corrections.
- Editorial brackets ([ ]) that appear in the score should not be transferred to the parts.
- If possible, include with your list of corrections a scan in PDF format of the first page of the score as well as the first page of the violin 1 and flute 1 parts. This will help identify materials, as sometimes publishers sell different printings of a work under the same plate/catalog number.
- When working with reprints, list the name of the original publisher on the header of the errata form. This information can be found on the reprint publisher's website or by contacting the reprint publisher directly. If you are unsure of the original publisher, avoid guesswork and leave the field blank; instead, include a scan as per above.

Abbreviations

Below are examples of a few common abbreviations. If you choose to use different abbreviations, please provide a key to their meaning on the first page of the errata form.

Symbol/Abbreviation	Meaning
[no symbol]	add
℈	delete
s/r	should read
stet	let it stand
m., mm.	measure, measures
b., db.	beat, downbeat
U, M, L	upper, middle, or lower line of a divisi section

Symbols

Music symbols can be used as an alternative to typing out long words or expressions. Specialized music fonts are not recommended as they can only be seen by users with these fonts installed on their computers. The symbols listed below can be seen by all users, as they are graphic representation of symbols, and they can be added to your computer's Clipboard, as follows:

- In Word 2003, access the Clipboard by selecting "Office Clipboard" from the Edit menu or hold down the "Ctrl" key while hitting the "C" key twice. In Word 2007, access the "Clipboard" from the Home menu.

- Add a symbol to your Clipboard by selecting the symbol below and hitting "Ctrl" + "C". Note: The Office Clipboard allows you to collect text and graphic items from any number of Office documents or other programs and then paste them into any Office document. The collected items stay on the Office Clipboard until you exit Office.
- Add the symbols to your document by placing the cursor where you want the symbol to appear and the then clicking on the symbol in the Clipboard.

MOLA ERRATA LIST
Corrections for Differences between Score and Parts

Page ___ of ___

Composer: _____   Original Publisher: _____

Title: _____   Reprint Publisher: _____

Arranger/Editor: _____   Plate Number: _____

Publication or © Date: _____   Reprint Date: _____

☐ Work entirely proofread   ☐ Work partially proofread   ☐ Errata found by players   ☐ Addendum to prior list

Additional information on the process of your proofreading of this piece:

_____

Number of Entries: _____

Notes

Please include information on alternate sources used, other available editions, quality of printing, previous proofreads, rehearsal systems (or lack thereof), page layout (including page turns) and any other information that will aid in the preparation of this work.

Status Codes	Abbreviations	
! = Critical correction. Some users of errata lists do not have time to make every correction listed. In order to help our colleagues save time, please identify the most important corrections.	no symbol	= add
	⅁	= remove
? = Requires a determination by librarian or conductor. In order to maintain consistency, the score matching the set of parts must be considered the primary reference. Any change from this point of reference must be documented when creating errata lists. When the score appears to be in error, corrections may involve the use of multiple references, performance practice, common sense, and/or opinion. Please list your reason for the change or document your other source(s).	s/r	= should read
	stet	= let it stand
	m., mm.	= measure, measures
	b., db.	= beat, downbeat
A blank cell indicates that this correction is not critical and/or does not require determination.	U, M, L	= upper, middle, or lower line of a divisi section

For an explanation of status codes and abbreviations, see the Errata section of www.mola-inc.org/
Submit completed lists to mola.errata@gmail.com
MOLA welcomes any additions, corrections, or comments to this errata list. MOLA claims no responsibility for the accuracy of any errata list.

Prepared by: *Organization:*   *Date:*

MOLA ERRATA LIST

Corrections for Differences between Score and Parts

Page ___ of ___

Composer: _____   Original Publisher: _____

Title: _____   Reprint Publisher: _____

Status	Instrument	Mvt.	Reh. Fig.	Meas. #	Beat	Correction

Prepared by: *Organization:*   *Date:*

Band Instrument Substitutions

There are occasions when you need to adapt another orchestration to be played by your band. It may be an arrangement for orchestra or brass band or a set of early band works without parts for saxophones or other "modern" instruments. The following are some suggestions for adapting other parts to a band instrumentation.

For this instrument...	use this part
Flute, Piccolo	1st Violin, Oboe; If possible, use a part in C although some old band sets will include D-flat or E-flat Flute or Piccolo parts
Oboe	Flute, 1st or 2nd Violin
E-flat Clarinet	E-flat Alto Saxophone, E-flat Cornet
1st B-flat Clarinet	1st or Solo Cornet
Section Clarinet	Occasionally marked "Ripieno" in some early editions
Alto Clarinet	E-flat Alto Saxophone, E-flat Cornet
Bass Clarinet	B-flat Tenor Saxophone, B-flat Baritone (treble clef), B-flat Tenor Horn
Alto Saxophone	E-flat Cornet
Tenor Saxophone	B-flat Baritone (treble clef), B-flat Tenor Horn
Baritone Saxophone	Bassoon, Baritone or Euphonium (bass clef), E-flat Bass
Trumpet	Cornet, Flügelhorn
Horn	E-flat Horns, Alto Horns (also known as Peck Horns)
Baritone (treble clef)	B-flat Tenor Saxophone, B-flat Tenor Horn
Euphonium	Cello, Tuba, Trombone, Bassoon
Tuba	Double Bass, Bassoon

For using band music of Great Britain, Italy, Spain, France, and Germany with American band instrumentation, see Appendix V, "Using foreign band music with American bands," in *The Heritage Encyclopedia of Band Music: Composers and Their Music* by William H. Rehrig, edited by Paul E. Bierley (Westerville, Ohio: Integrity Press, 1991), 869–870.

For instructions on how one instrument can play another's part using the "clef substitution method," see *Guide to Score Study for the Wind Band Conductor* by Frank L. Battisti and Robert J. Garofalo (Ft. Lauderdale, Fla: Meredith Music Publications, 1990), 73–78.

For a list of percussion instrument substitutions, see "Substitute Percussion Instruments," by James McKinney in *The Instrumentalist* 34, no. 12 (July 1980): 41–42, or "Percussion Instrument Substitution: A Practical Necessity," by Mario Gaetano, available online at http://chaptersites.pas.org/NorthCarolina/psubs.htm.

APPENDIX

A

LIBRARY FORMS

The following are examples of typical library forms in a couple of different formats. Feel free to reproduce these forms for use in your library. Two of the forms have samples to illustrate their use.

1. Performance Library Cataloging Form
2. Performance Library Cataloging Form with sample data
3. Cataloging Information
4. Band Library Inventory
5. Band Cataloging Form
6. Orchestra Cataloging Form
7. Orchestra Library Inventory
8. Big Band Cataloging Form
9. Music Preparation Form
10. Music Preparation Checklist
11. Music Preparation Checklist with sample data
12. Bowing Assignments
13. Performance Record

PDFs of these forms can be downloaded from:
http://www.girsberger.us/Library/LIBRARY_FORMS.html

Performance Library Cataloging Form

Box no. _____

Composer _____

Composer 2 _____

Arranger/Editor _____

Title 1 _____

Title 2 _____

Publisher _____ © date _____

Plate no. _____ Duration _____

Edition no. _____ Collection _____

Notes _____

Fl ☐ _____	Hp ☐	V1 ☐
Ob ☐ _____	Kb ☐	V2 ☐
Cl ☐ _____		Va ☐
Bn ☐ _____		Vc ☐
Hn ☐ _____	Solo Instruments ☐	Cb ☐
Tp ☐ _____		
Tb ☐ _____	Other ☐	Notes
Tu ☐ _____		
T ☐ _____		
Perc ☐		

WBP Total Players ☐   **WBP** Total Parts ☐

Performance Library Cataloging Form

Box no. _____425_____

Composer	Strauss, Johann, Jr.
Composer 2	
Arranger/Editor	
Title 1	Voices of Spring, op. 410
Title 2	Frühlingsstimmen Walzer, op. 410
Publisher	Breitkopf & Härtel (Leipzig) © date n.d.
Plate no.	Orch. B. 2757 Duration 6:00
Edition no.	Orchesterbibliothek Nr. 2757 Collection Orchestra
Notes	Bowings from Philharmonic. Rehearsal letters and bar count.

Fl	2	1, P		Hp	1		V1	7
Ob	2	1, 2		Kb			V2	6
Cl	2	1, 2 (Bb)					Va	5
Bn	2	1, 2					Vc	4
Hn	4	1, 2, 3, 4 (F)		Solo Instruments			Cb	3
Tp	2	1, 2 (F)						
Tb	3	1, 2, 3						
Tu				Other			Notes	
T	1	1						
Perc	2							

Kleine und Große Trommel
[Snare drum, bass drum]

WBP Total Players 21   **WBP** Total Parts 21

CATALOGING INFORMATION

COMPOSER

TITLE

PUBLISHER / COPYRIGHT HOLDER

REMARKS

CATALOG NUMBER

TIMING

COPYRIGHT DATE

INSTRUMENTATION

1st VIOLIN	FLUTE
2nd VIOLIN	OBOE
VIOLA	CLARINET
CELLO	BASSOON
BASS	HORN

TRUMPET

HARP
PIANO

TROMBONE

TUBA

TIMPANI

PERCUSSION:

ADDITIONAL INSTRUMENTS:

BAND LIBRARY INVENTORY

INVENTORY DATE

Full Score
1st and 2nd Flute
Oboe
1st Clarinet
2nd Clarinet
3rd Clarinet
Bass Clarinet
Bassoon
Alto Saxophone
Tenor Saxophone
Baritone Saxophone
1st Trumpet
2nd Trumpet
3rd Trumpet
1st and 2nd Horns
3rd and 4th Horns
1st Trombone
2nd Trombone
3rd Trombone
Baritone (Treble Clef)
Baritone (Bass Clef)
Tuba
Tympani

PERFORMANCE RECORD

Date	Occasion	Date	Occasion

BAND CATALOGING FORM

Title _____ Catalog No. _____

Composer _____ Set No. _____

Arranger / Editor _____

Publisher _____

Copyright Holder _____ Copyright Date _____

Plate No. _____ Edition No. _____ Duration_____

Notes _____

_____ Full Score	_____ Bassoon 1	_____ Trombone 1
_____ Condensed Score	_____ Bassoon 2	_____ Trombone 2
_____ Solo Part	_____ Bassoon 3	_____ Trombone 3
_____ _____	_____ Bassoon 4	_____ Trombone 4
_____ _____	_____ Contrabassoon	_____ _____
_____ Flute 1	_____ _____	_____ Baritone (Treble Clef)
_____ Flute 2	_____ Soprano Sax	_____ Euphonium (Bass Clef)
_____ Flute 3	_____ Alto Sax 1	_____ _____
_____ Flute 4	_____ Alto Sax 2	_____ Tuba 1
_____ C Piccolo	_____ Tenor Sax	_____ Tuba 2
_____ Db Piccolo	_____ Baritone Sax	_____ _____
_____ _____	_____ _____	_____ Double Bass
_____ _____	_____ _____	_____ _____
_____ Oboe 1	_____ Horn 1	_____ Timpani
_____ Oboe 2	_____ Horn 2	_____ Percussion _____
_____ Oboe 3	_____ Horn 3	_____ _____
_____ Oboe 4	_____ Horn 4	_____ _____
_____ English Horn	_____ _____	_____ _____
_____ _____	_____ _____	_____ _____
_____ _____	_____ Eb Cornet	_____ Harp 1
_____ Eb Clarinet	_____ Solo Cornet	_____ Harp 2
_____ Solo Clarinet	_____ Cornet 1	_____ Piano
_____ Clarinet 1	_____ Cornet 2	_____ Celeste
_____ Clarinet 2	_____ Cornet 3	_____ Organ
_____ Clarinet 3	_____ Cornet 4	_____ Synthesizer
_____ Clarinet 4	_____ _____	_____ _____
_____ Alto Clarinet	_____ Trumpet 1	_____ Guitar
_____ Bass Clarinet	_____ Trumpet 2	_____ Bass Guitar
_____ Eb Contrabass Clarinet	_____ Trumpet 3	_____ _____
_____ Bb Contrabass Clarinet	_____ Trumpet 4	_____ _____
_____ _____	_____ Flügelhorn	_____ _____
_____ _____	_____ _____	_____ _____

x

ORCHESTRA CATALOGING FORM

Title _____ Catalog No. _____

Composer _____ Set No. _____

Arranger / Editor _____

Publisher _____

Copyright Holder _____ Copyright Date _____

Plate No. _____ Edition No. _____ Duration _____

Notes _____

____ Full Score	____ Bassoon 1	____ Trombone 1
____ Condensed Score	____ Bassoon 2	____ Trombone 2
____ Solo Part	____ Bassoon 3	____ Trombone 3
____ _____	____ Bassoon 4	____ Trombone 4
____ Violin 1 (A)	____ Contrabassoon	____ _____
____ Violin 2 (B)	____ _____	____ Tenor Tuba
____ Violin 3 (C)	____ Soprano Sax	____ Tuba 1
____ Viola	____ Alto Sax	____ Tuba 2
____ Cello	____ Tenor Sax	____ _____
____ Bass	____ Baritone Sax	____ _____
____ _____	____ _____	____ Timpani 1
____ _____	____ _____	____ Timpani 2
____ Flute 1	____ Horn 1	____ Percussion _____
____ Flute 2	____ Horn 2	____ _____
____ Flute 3	____ Horn 3	____ _____
____ Flute 4	____ Horn 4	____ _____
____ Piccolo	____ Horn 5	____ _____
____ _____	____ Horn 6	____ Harp 1
____ Oboe 1	____ Horn 7	____ Harp 2
____ Oboe 2	____ Horn 8	____ Piano
____ Oboe 3	____ _____	____ Celeste
____ Oboe 4	____ Trumpet 1	____ Organ
____ English Horn	____ Trumpet 2	____ Harpsichord
____ _____	____ Trumpet 3	____ Synthesizer
____ Clarinet 1	____ Trumpet 4	____ _____
____ Clarinet 2	____ Trumpet 5	____ Guitar
____ Clarinet 3	____ Trumpet 6	____ Bass Guitar
____ Clarinet 4	____ Cornet 1	____ _____
____ E♭ Clarinet	____ Cornet 2	____ _____
____ Bass Clarinet	____ Cornet 3	____ _____
____ _____	____ _____	____ _____

Orchestra Library Inventory

Composer _____

Title _____   Catalog no. ____

___ Flute I.
___ Flute II.
___ Flute III.
___ Flute IV.
___ Piccolo
_____
_____

___ Oboe I.
___ Oboe II.
___ Oboe III.
___ Oboe IV.
___ English Horn
_____

___ Clarinet I.
___ Clarinet II.
___ Clarinet III.
___ Clarinet IV.
___ Eb Clarinet
___ Bass Clarinet
_____
_____

___ Bassoon I.
___ Bassoon II.
___ Bassoon III.
___ Bassoon IV.
___ Contra Bassoon

___ Soprano Sax
___ Alto Sax
___ Tenor Sax
_____
_____
_____
_____

___ Horn I.
___ Horn II.
___ Horn III.
___ Horn IV.
___ Horn V.
___ Horn VI.
___ Horn VII.
___ Horn VIII.

___ Wagner Tuben I.
___ Wagner Tuben II.
___ Wagnre Tuben III.
___ Wagner Tuben IV.

___ Trumpet I.
___ Trumpet II.
___ Trumpet III.
___ Trumpet IV.
_____
_____
_____

___ Trombone I.
___ Trombone II.
___ Trombone III.
___ Trombone IV.
___ Bass Trombone
___ Euphonium (Tenor Tuba)

___ Tuba I.
___ Tuba II.
_____
_____
_____

___ Timpani I.
___ Timpani II.

___ Percussion
_____
_____
_____
_____
_____
_____
_____

___ Harp I.
___ Harp II.

___ Piano
___ Celeste
___ Organ
___ Keyboard I.
___ Keyboard II.

Miscellaneous
_____
_____
_____
_____
_____
_____

Strings

___ Violin I.
___ Violin II.
___ Viola
___ Cello
___ Bass

Additional Strings
_____
_____
_____

BIG BAND CATALOGING FORM

Title _____ Catalog No. _____

Composer _____

Arranger / Transcriber_____

Publisher _____

Copyright Holder _____Copyright Date _____

Solos _____ Style_____ Duration_____

Notes _____

_____ Full Score	_____ Trumpet 1	_____ Piano
_____ Condensed Score	_____ Trumpet 2	_____ Keyboard
_____ Lead Sheet	_____ Trumpet 3	_____ Synthesizer
_____ Solo Part	_____ Trumpet 4	_____ Acoustic Bass
_____ _____	_____ Trumpet 5	_____ Electric Bass
_____ _____	_____ Solo Trumpet	_____ Guitar
_____ _____	_____ _____	_____ _____
_____ _____	_____ _____	_____ _____
_____ Soprano Sax	_____ _____	_____ Drum Set
_____ 1st Alto Sax	_____ Trombone 1	_____ Vibraphone
_____ 2nd Alto Sax	_____ Trombone 2	_____ Auxiliary Percussion
_____ 1st Tenor Sax	_____ Trombone 3	_____ _____
_____ 2nd Tenor Sax	_____ Trombone 4	_____ _____
_____ Baritone Sax	_____ Bass Trombone	_____ _____
_____ _____	_____ Tuba	_____ _____
_____ _____	_____ _____	_____ _____
_____ _____	_____ _____	_____ _____
_____ Reed 1 _____	_____ _____	
_____ Reed 2 _____		
_____ Reed 3 _____		
_____ Reed 4 _____		
_____ Reed 5 _____		
_____ _____		
_____ _____		
_____ _____		
_____ _____		

Music Preparation Form

Composer _____

Title _____

Ensemble _____

Performance date _____   Venue _____

Date Due _____   Contacted conductor _____

First Rehearsal _____   _____

Date Ready _____   _____

Acquisitions   Publisher / Source _____

☐ *In Library*   Box no. _____   Scores _____

_____   _____

☐ *Sales*   Ordered _____   ☐ *Rental*   Ordered _____

Due _____   Due _____

Rec'd _____   Rec'd _____

_____   Contract _____

_____   _____

_____   _____

_____   _____

Part Preparation   *Done*   *Done*

Bowings _____ ☐   Clean _____ ☐

_____   Practice parts _____ ☐

Masters _____ To bowmarkers _____   Page turns _____ ☐

Due _____   Ready _____   Other _____ ☐

Errata _____ ☐   _____ ☐

Repair _____ ☐   _____ ☐

Notes

Composer	Title	Source	Notes

Orchestra — Fall 2007

Composer	Title	Own/Rent/Purchase	Source	Ordered	Received	Clean & Repair	Bowings	Performance parts	Practice parts	Dep'l/asst scores	Due date	Ready	Notes
October 31, 2007													
Bartók	Concerto for Orchestra	O	Boosey	9/10	9/21	√	√	√	√	√	10/9	10/8	
November 7, 2007													
Tchaikovsky	Symphony No. 4	O	T-105										
November 14, 2007													
Berlioz	Symphonie Fantastique	O	B-690										
November 26, 2007													
Verdi	La Forza del Destino: Overture	O	V-25										
Verdi	Nabucco: Overture	O	V-33										
Rossini	La Gazza Ladra: Overture	O	R-145										
December 12, 2007													
Mahler	Symphony No. 6 — Finale	O	M-37										

Bowing Assignments

Date due: _____

Title _____

Orchestra/ Concert Date _____

Please initial and date below when you take the parts from the library.

1st Violin _____   Winds _____

2nd Violin _____   Brass _____

Viola _____   Percussion _____

Cello _____   _____

Bass _____   _____

Notes:

PERFORMANCE RECORD

Date	Ensemble	Conductor	Event

APPENDIX

B

GLOSSARY

accession number: A number assigned to an item that identifies its shelf location and/or the order in which it was acquired.

acid-free: Paper or paper materials having a pH measurement of 7.0 or greater on a scale of 0 to 14. Materials with a lower number have a greater acid content, while a higher number indicates a greater alkaline content.

arrangement: The reworking of a musical composition, usually for a different medium than that of the original, which often involves altering the harmony, rhythm, accompaniment figures, and orchestration. Compare with transcription.

arranger: The person who writes the *arrangement*.

audition list: A list of music selections or excerpts to be performed at an audition for a job or an ensemble placement.

authority: A resource used to establish the form and spelling of a title or name. Authority records document variant forms of the heading and identify the pre-ferred form of a heading to use in the library catalog. Established authority files for libraries are supported by the Library of Congress (http://authorities.loc.gov).

autograph: A manuscript document written in the hand of an author who can be identified. See also *holograph*.

back stand: The music stands in the rear of a string section, and/or the music folders and parts on those stands.

banda: (It.) The group of musicians whose playing is part of the action in an opera, either onstage (in costume) or offstage behind the scenes. Examples are found in Mozart's *Don Giovanni*, Verdi's *Rigoletto*, and others. Also known as "stage band."

bar count: Measure numbers written or printed in a part or score.

bibliographic description: A text representation of a document, book, or item. It includes such information as the creator, title, publication date, physical dimen-sions, content, and format.

bowing masters: One copy of each string part, either an original or a photocopy, that shows the bowings used by a particular orchestra, conductor, or concertmaster. The string masters are used as a guide to hand copy those particular bowings into another set of parts.

bowings: Indications in music for string instruments that instruct the player to use a down bow stroke or an up bow stroke.

collection: Three or more independent works gathered together in a single publica-tion. The collection will contain complete versions of the works, usually brought together by some unifying topic such as Christmas Carols for Brass Quintet or Sousa March Book. See also *medley* and *selections*.

critical edition: A publication intended to be the most accurate to the composer's intentions, derived by examining and comparing primary source materials. More information about creating such an edition can be cound in "Scholarly editions: their character and bibliographic description," by Keith E. Mixter, published in *Foundations in Music Bibliography*, edited by Richard D. Green (New York: Haworth Press, 1993).

desk: See *stand*.

divisi: (It., abbreviation: div.) An indication that an instrumental line is divided into two or more parts, to be performed by separate players, frequently found in string parts but occasionally seen in music for winds and brass.

doubling: In a music performance, this refers to a musician playing one or more instruments in addition to their primary instrument during a composition or a concert. In terms of orchestration, doubling can also refer to the practice of two players performing the same part simultaneously. Some conductors will double woodwind parts to reinforce the music and the sound of a specific instrument.

duplex: A photocopy machine feature which allows the copier to print on both sides of the page.

edition: All copies produced from the same master copy or printing plates and issued by the same publisher.

edition number: See *publisher's number*.

editor: A person who prepares an item for publication that is not his or her own creation. The editing may consist of gathering the material for publication, adding notes or critical matter, or musicological supervision and alteration of the material.

errata: Errors and their corrections found in music or text. Errata lists are used to record and disseminate this information among conductors, players, and librarians.

excerpt: A portion of a complete work, often requested on an audition list. Published excerpts books gather together representative excerpts for an instrument as an aid for audition preparation or study.

facsimile: A reproduction intended to simulate the physical appearance of the original, while reproducing its content exactly.

fan-fold: A method of taping part pages so that each single-sided page is taped to the next in sequence and all lay face up in a row.

holograph: A manuscript document, score, or musical part written entirely in the hand of its creator. See also *autograph*.

in tono: (It.) In the original key, seen in opera parts with alternate transpositions of arias. See also the related term *transporto*.

leaf: A single sheet of paper comprising two pages, one on each side. The front side is the *recto* and the back side is the *verso*.

manuscript: A handwritten or typescript document; an unpublished document.

march-size: A term identifying the size of a music edition, measuring approximately 5×7 inches. Music printed at this size is intended to be used by marching bands in parades or field shows and is sized to fit on an instrument's music lyre or in a marching flip folder. Also identified as quickstep size.

medley: Three or more independent works, from disparate sources, gathered together in a composition under a single title. For example: Star Spangled Spectacular: The Music of George M. Cohan. See also *collection* and *selections*.

MOLA: Acronym of the Major Orchestra Librarians' Association, the professional organization for performance librarians. Information about MOLA can be found on their website, http://www.mola-inc.org.

octavo: A term identifying the size of the music, measuring approximately 7 × 10½ inches. Choral music is usually printed in octavo size, as were many early band and dance orchestra compositions.

on deposit: A set of rental parts that is retained by a performing ensemble. The sets usually contain bowings and performance markings unique to the ensemble or the conductor which the organization wants to preserve for their future use.

orchestra set (A, B, or C): A publisher's term to identify a set of parts for sale, usually distinguished by the number of string parts included in each size, A being the smallest and C being the largest.

page: One side of a *leaf*.

part (or parts): A piece of music intended to be played by one of the voices or instruments in a musical work. See also *set*.

perusal score: A score offered on loan by a publisher for the purpose of research, study, or examination for consideration of performance.

pH: A measure of the acidity or alkalinity of paper. See also *acid-free*.

plate number: A numerical or alpha-numerical identification assigned to an item by a music publisher, usually printed at the bottom of each page of music, used to identify a specific musical work in their catalog or the printing plates used to produce it.

proof, proofed, proofing: A form of the word "proofreading," indicating examination of the music to identify errors or errata in printing, identified by comparing two or more sources.

publisher's number: A numerical or alpha-numerical identification assigned to an item or set of items by a music publisher, usually appearing on the cover, title page, or first page of music, used to identify a specific musical work in their catalog. Sometimes known as edition number.

pulte: (Ger.) Desk or stand. This often refers to two string players, siting at the same music stand, reading music from the same part, and is often used when indicating divisi instructions.

public domain: Works in the public domain are no longer protected by the copyright law and as such may be reproduced, edited, or arranged without the approval of, or payment to, the copyright holder.

quarto: A term identifying the size of the music, measuring approximately 10 × 13 inches.

quickstep: See *march-size*.

recto: The right-hand page of a book or piece of music, usually bearing an odd-page number.

relative humidity: A measurement of the amount of moisture in the air, expressed as a percentage of the amount of water vapor in the air compared to the amount the air could hold if it was totally saturated.

reprint publisher: Companies that publish editions of music that are in the *public domain* or no longer protected by the copyright law. They reproduce these editions, replacing the original publisher's name with their own, and sell the music.

score: A piece of music that shows all the voices and/or instruments in the composition. The musical staves are arranged vertically to show what parts play simultaneously. Scores come in different formats and sizes for specific purposes. For examples, see the article "Score Identification."

score-form percussion part: A part which includes all the instrumental voices for the percussion section (although not always including timpani), preferred by some players because it allows them to see all instruments simultaneously and divide player assignments according to their own numbers and needs.

score order: The order of instruments as they appear from the top of the page to the bottom in a conductor's full score. Typically the order is woodwinds, brass, percussion, harp, keyboards, solo instruments, and strings. For examples, see the article "Score Order."

selections: Three or more independent works from the same larger work, gathered together in a composition under a single title. For example: Highlights from *The Music Man*. See also *collection* and *medley*.

service: A musical activity or event that involves the players and often the library staff. Services are usually considered to include rehearsals, concerts, recording sessions, and other events as agreed upon by the ensemble or organization.

set (or set of parts): All of the individual parts that are needed to perform a musical work. For example, a set of parts for an orchestra consists of at least one of each part written for the wind, brass, percussion, harp, and keyboard instrumentalists, and enough copies of each of the string parts (1st and 2nd violin, viola, cello, double bass) for the entire section.

signature: A gathering of pages ready for binding, created when large sheet of paper is folded in half. When the folds are cut, they make four (or a multiple of four) individual pages.

sitzprobe: (Ger.) Literally, "sitting rehearsal." A purely musical rehearsal of an opera, without stage action, in which singers perform with orchestral accompaniment for the first time.

staff: A series of lines (typically 5 horizontal lines) on which music is notated. Also known as stave. Two or more staffs joined together are known as a *system*.

stage band: See *banda*.

stand: With regard to ensemble seating, a stand indicates where a player is seated, such as "first stand clarinet" or "second stand trumpet." In the string section, a stand usually refers to both players that share the stand, such as "first stand viola" or "last stand cello." Also known as desk.

stand number: For string instruments, the number given to a part that is played by a specific stand of players in each section, such as 1st Violin [stand] 1, 1st Violin [stand] 2, etc. By numbering the parts, each stand will get the same part used at the previous performance, with all the cues and divisi markings appropriate to that stand of players.

stave: See *staff*.

string count: A number indicating how many music stands are used in each string section of an orchestra, given in the following order: 1st violins, 2nd violins, violas, cellos, basses. Thus a string count of "8 7 6 5 4" indicates 8 stands of 1st violins, 7 stands of 2nd violins, 6 stands of violas, 5 stands of cellos, and 4 stands of basses. The string count can be used when ordering parts or when communicating the size of a string section. Fractions may be used to indicate a single player on a stand (8 6½ 5 4 3). The number tells how many single copies of each instrumental part are needed for the performance (given one part for each stand). In some organizations or compositions, these numbers may indicate the player count (16 13 10 8 6).

string masters: See *bowing masters*.

symphonic band: A music publishing term identifying an enlarged sale edition of band music which offers additional parts not included in the regular band set, such as Alto Clarinet, E-flat Horns, or Double Bass.

system: One or more music *staves*, usually grouped together with a brace or bracket in the left margin.

tacet sheet: A sheet of paper which acts as a placeholder to indicate that no music was written for a specific instrument in a given composition.

transliteration: As applied to opera libretti, it involves mapping the letters of the source script to letters pronounounced similarly in the goal script. For example, a text in Cyrillic will be written in Roman characters that should result in the word sounding the same despite being written in an different alphabet.

transcription: The translation of a musical composition for another ensemble or medium, without altering the melodic, harmonic, or rhythmic structure, form, or musical substance of the original work. Compare with *arrangement*.

transporto: (It.) In the transposed key, seen in opera parts as alternate transpositions of arias. See also the related term *in tono*.

uniform title: A standardized form of a title by which a work is identified for cataloging purposes. It is used to bring together all the catalog records of the same work that are published or labeled with different forms of the title.

urtext edition: A modern edition of a work that reproduces the earliest version, free of editorial additions.

verso: The left-hand page of a book or piece of music, usually bearing an even page number.

vide: (Latin) See; When the word is divided and written in a score or part, it will indicate the beginning (vi-) and ending (-de) of a portion of music to be "cut" or omitted in performance.

wandelprobe (*wandel*): (Ger.) The first staged rehearsal of an opera, where the singers practice their blocking and stage movements, accompanied by the orchestra in the pit.

Thanks to Robert Sutherland and John Yaffé for assistance with this glossary.

APPENDIX

C

BIBLIOGRAPHY

Chapter 1: Library Basics

ONLINE RESOURCES

Major Orchestra Librarians' Association: http://www.mola-inc.org

> The organization's website gives information about MOLA activities, job announcements, articles about the profession, back issues of the Association's newsletter, and links to publisher and composer web pages.

Symphony Orchestra Library Center: http://www.orchestralibrary.com

> Operated by Steven Sherrill of the Atlanta Symphony, this site includes helpful lists of typical audition repertoire for all instruments, transposed orchestral parts, and many links to Internet resources on topics from performing organizations to library preservation.

Orchestra Library Information: http://launch.groups.yahoo.com/group/OrchLibInfo/ ?yguid=137775693

> A chat and message exchange group to post questions and share information about orchestral repertoire and performance library practices and procedures. Moderated by Thomas Pease (Library of Congress) and Clinton F. Nieweg (The Philadelphia Orchestra, retired).

Polyphonic.org. The Orchestra Musician Forum: http://www.polyphonic.org

> Founded by Paul R. Judy and operated by the Eastman School of Music, this site includes articles on all aspects of orchestral performance. The Music Librarian forum is moderated by Karen Schnackenberg (Dallas Symphony), who also writes a blog for the site.

LIBRARY MANUALS AND PRACTICES

Byrne, Frank P., Jr. *A Practical Guide to the Music Library: Its Function, Organization and Maintenance*. Cleveland, Ohio: Ludwig Music, 1987. A detailed manual covering classification and cataloging, authority work, and music care, repair, and archival considerations. The twenty-three appendices include reproducible library forms.

———. "What's in a Name?" *BD Guide* 8, no. 1 (September–October 1993): 6–7. Suggestions for developing composer-title authority control in your ensemble library catalog. Available online at http://www.mola-inc.org in the Press Room.

Delacoma, Wynne. "Turning the Page." *Symphony* 59, no. 1 (January-February 2008): 57–62. A look at the use of digital technology (scanners, copiers, notation software) in the performance library. Available online at http://www.mola-inc.org in the Press Room.

Dougan, Kirstin. *A Guide to the Orchestra Library*. Madison, Wis.: the author [Music and Performing Arts Library, University of Illinois, Urbana, IL 61801, e-mail: dougan@illinois.edu], 1998. Intended for the community or university orchestra librarian, this manual presents basic library practices, including acquiring and preparing music, cataloging, and record keeping.

Girsberger, Russ. *A Manual for the Performance Library.* Music Library Association Basic Manual Series, No. 6. Lanham, Md.: Scarecrow Press, 2006. A broad view of performance library processes and responsibilities.

Gittinger Farabee, Marcia. "Commissions & Consortiums: Working Together." *Progressions* [American Symphony Orchestra League] 3, no. 2 (January 1992): 4. The third in a series of four articles by the librarian of the National Symphony Orchestra addresses the preparation of composer commission and consortium agreements. Available online at http://www.mola-inc.org in the Press Room.

――――. "Do You Know Where Your License Is?" *Progressions* [American Symphony Orchestra League] 3, no. 1 (October 1991): 3–4. The second article in the series discusses copyright and performing rights, with an overview of the law and the function of ASCAP and BMI. Available online at http://www.mola-inc.org in the Press Room.

――――. "Questions and Answers From an Orchestra Librarian." *Progressions* [American Symphony Orchestra League] 3, no. 3 (April 1992): 3. The final article in the series answers common questions about bowing, photocopying, copyright, and the profession of orchestral librarianship. Available online at http://www. mola-inc.org in the Press Room.

Kloss, Marilyn Bone. *Handbook for Community Orchestra Librarians.* Concord, Mass.: the author [1 Concord Greene #8, Concord, MA 01742, e-mail: mbkloss@comcast.net], 1999. This monograph provides details on budgeting, music acquisition, part preparation, and workflow, with some discussion of copyright responsibilities and working with rental music.

Nieweg, Clinton F., and Robert Sutherland. "Editions Paper." Paper read at the International Association of Music Librarians (IAML) meeting, Wellington, New Zealand, July 1999. Subtitled, "A discussion of various editorial trends and how a conductor's decision to use a particular edition may impact the librarian." An overview of the process to create critical editions and how those scholarly work may not be practical as performing editions. Available online at http://www.mola-inc.org/PressRoom/EditionspaperJuly1999.pdf.

Tarlow, Lawrence, and Robert Sutherland. "The Music We Perform: An Overview of Royalties, Rentals and Rights." Rev. ed. n.p.: Major Orchestra Librarians' Association, 2004. Librarians from the New York Philharmonic and The Metropolitan Opera explain copyright as it relates to performing materials for rent and in the public domain. Includes an explanation of simple and grand rights as they relate to performing ensembles. Available online at http://www.mola-inc.org/pdf/MusicWePerform.pdf.

CAREER INFORMATION

"Behind the Scenes: A Roundtable." *Harmony* no. 9 (October 1999): 61–71. A five-way interview organized by the Symphony Orchestra Institute with orchestra librarians Marcia Farabee (National Symphony), Margo Hodgson (Winnipeg Symphony), Karen Schnackenberg (Dallas Symphony), Larry Tarlow (New York Philharmonic), and Ron Whitaker (Cleveland Orchestra). They discuss the requirements and responsibilities of the job and the function of the library within the orchestra structure. Available online at http://www.soi.org/harmony/archive/9/Behind_Scenes_SOI.pdf.

Burlingame, Marshall. "Concert Production's New Ally: A Computer Learns the Score." *Symphony Magazine* 34, no. 1 (February–March 1983): 11–13. This article prefaced the introduction of the OLIS computer software application for orchestra administration control. The author identifies the numerous bits of repertoire, performance details, and non-musical information that can be gathered into a database for use by librarians, conductors, personnel managers, and stage managers. Available online at http://www.mola-inc.org in the Press Room.

———. "Staging an Orchestra Concert." *MadAminA* [Music Associates of America] 4, no. 1 (Spring 1983): 13–15. A look at the many behind-the-scenes activities involved in preparing a performance, from the perspectives of the librarian, personnel manager, and music director. Available online at http://musicassociatesofamerica.com/madamina/1983/staging.html.

Gittinger Farabee, Marcia. "Getting the Most From your Orchestra Librarian." *Progressions* [American Symphony Orchestra League] 2, no. 4 (August 1991): 3. A broad look at the responsibilities of the orchestra librarian and their importance to the organization, along with a list of necessary equipment for the library. Available online at http://www.mola-inc.org in the Press Room.

Holmes, Andrew S. "Classification of the performance librarian within the orchestra." B.A. thesis paper. Madison, N.J.: Drew University, 1998. This study of the musical and administrative duties of a performance librarian is drawn from interviews with over twenty professional librarians. Holmes also summarizes the librarian's position within each orchestra's administrative structure. Available online at http://www.mola-inc.org in the Press Room.

Major Orchestra Librarians' Association. "The Orchestra Librarian, A Career Introduction." n.p.: Major Orchestra Librarians' Association, 1992. A brief overview of the role of performance librarians in orchestra, opera, and ballet music, and training opportunities for the profession. Available online at http://www.mola-inc.org/orchlib.html.

Schnackenberg, Karen. "Walking in Two Worlds: A Librarian's Perspective." *Harmony* no. 16 (October 2003): 123–131. The performance librarian has responsibilities to the "two worlds" of their organization: the musicians and the administration. Schnackenberg also describes a music acquisition campaign that helped raise funds for library music purchases. Available online at http://www.soi.org/harmony/archive/16/Librarian_Schnackenberg.pdf.

Chapter 2: Acquisitions

BIBLIOGRAPHIES OF MUSIC
Other bibliographies of music are listed in the article "Resources for Cataloging."

ORCHESTRA

American Society of Composers, Authors and Publishers. *ASCAP Symphonic Catalog*. 3rd ed. New York: R. R. Bowker, 1977. Supplement, 1981. A catalog of compositions with United States performing rights held by ASCAP, listing instrumentation, publisher, and duration. The ASCAP website (http://www.ascap.com/ace) has a searchable database to identify the rights holder of their licensed songs and a second database of works that have been restored to copyright protection as a result of the GATT treaty (http://www.ascap.com/restored_works/restore_index.cfm).

British Broadcasting Corporation, Central Music Library. *Orchestral Catalogue*. Edited by Shelia Compton. London: British Broadcasting Corporation, 1982. 4 volumes. The printed catalogs of the BBC radio music library. Although not a lending library, the catalogs are a useful resource to identify published editions of small and large ensemble music.

Broadcast Music, Inc. *BMI Symphonic Catalog*. Rev. ed. New York: BMI, 1971. Supplement, 1978. A catalog of compositions with United States performing rights held by BMI. The BMI website has a searchable database to identify the rights holder of their licensed songs at http://www.bmi.com.

Butterworth, Neil. *Neglected Music: A Repertoire Handbook for Orchestras and Choirs*. London: Robert Hale, 1991. Butterworth recommends lesser-known works by major composers in the choral, orchestral, solo instrument with orchestral accompaniment, string orchestra, and opera repertoires.

The Edwin A. Fleisher Collection of Orchestral Music in the Free Library of Philadelphia: A Cumulative Catalog, 1929–1977. Boston: G. K. Hall, 1979. A catalog of over 4,000 pieces of orchestra music available on loan from the Free Library. It is also a useful guide for locating obscure or out of print music. The catalog can be searched online at http://libwww.library.phila.gov/collections/collectionDetail.cfm?id=14.

OPERA AND MUSICAL THEATER

British Broadcasting Corporation, Central Music Library. *Choral and Opera Catalogue*. London: British Broadcasting Corporation, 1967. 2 volumes. The printed catalogs of the BBC radio music library.

Lubbock, Mark. *The Complete Book of Light Opera*. American Section by David Ewen. London: Putnam; New York: Appleton-Century-Crofts, 1962. Lubbock focuses on operettas by Gilbert and Sullivan, Victor Herbert, Offenbach, Lehar, Sousa, and others, as well as some entries that could be considered musical theater works. He includes production information, cast list, synopsis by act, and musical incipits, although not always song or aria titles.

Lucha-Burns, Carol. *Musical Notes: A Practical Guide to Staffing and Staging Standards of the American Musical Theatre*. New York: Greenwood Press, 1986. The best guide to production details of American musical theater works, including staging, costuming, orchestration, and contact information for script, music, and performing rights sources.

Martin, George. *The Opera Companion: A Guide for the Casual Operagoer*. New York: Dodd, Mead and Co., 1961.

———. *The Companion to Twentieth-Century Opera*. New York: Dodd, Mead and Co., 1979.

The Opera Companion includes information on fifty 17th- and 18th-century operas (published in paperback as Volume 2), while *Twentieth-Century Opera* examines ninety-eight works. Each article includes a synopsis, act timings, cast list, and occasionally aria titles. Both books contain interesting essays and other useful appendices.

BAND AND WIND ENSEMBLE

Clark, David Lindsey. *Appraisals of Original Wind Music: A Survey and Guide*. Music Reference Collection Series, 77. Westport, Conn.: Greenwood Press, 1999. A catalog of wind chamber music, delineated into solo and small ensemble works, with descriptive analysis of significant works and lists of related repertoire at the end of each chapter.

CHORAL MUSIC

British Broadcasting Corporation, Central Music Library. *Choral and Opera Catalogue*. London: British Broadcasting Corporation, 1967. 2 volumes. The printed catalogs of the BBC radio music library.

CHAMBER MUSIC

British Broadcasting Corporation, Central Music Library. *Chamber Music Catalogue*. London: British Broadcasting Corporation, 1965. The printed catalog of the BBC radio music library.

Cobbett, Walter Wilson, compiler and editor. *Cyclopedia Survey of Chamber Music*. 2nd ed. London: Oxford University Press, 1963. 3 volumes. A classic reference work, it is strong on 18th- and 19th-century repertoire for three to nine instruments, while the third volume updates the work and corrects errors in the first two volumes.

Cohn, Arthur. *The Literature of Chamber Music*. Chapel Hill, N.C.: Hinshaw Music, 1997. A four-volume encyclopedia of chamber music repertoire. The entries are arranged by composer, then title, each with the instrumentation and a brief essay about the work, but no publisher information.

Hinson, Maurice, and Wesley Roberts. *The Piano in Chamber Ensemble: An Annotated Guide*. Bloomington, Ind.: Indiana University Press, 2006. Examines works from two to eight players that includes the piano on an equal basis as the other instruments. Most entries include technical and musical description of the work, in addition to publication information.

Rangel-Ribeiro, Victor, and Robert Markel. *Chamber Music: An International Guide to Works and Their Instrumentation*. New York: Facts on File, 1993. A list of music from the pre-Baroque to 1992, arranged in a chart format to indicate the instrumentation of the selected works. The charts also include date of publication or composition, duration, and publisher information.

Winchester, Barbara, and Kay Dunlap. *Vocal Chamber Music: A Performer's Guide*. New York: Routledge, 2008. A catalog of works for at least one voice and one instrument up to twelve voices and twelve instruments. The compositions must date from 1650 to 1980 and have been in print at the time of publication.

POPULAR MUSIC

Lax, Roger, and Frederick Smith. *The Great Song Thesaurus*. 2nd ed. New York: Oxford University Press, 1989. A handy, one-volume guide to international popular song from the 1400s to 1986. Includes helpful additional lists of song titles by subject and category, award winners, and theme and signature songs.

Popular Music. Detroit, Mich.: Gale Research, 1988–. A series of books outlining popular songs and musical trends from 1900 to the present. They are published annually and also in compilation volumes. Each volume includes an essay on music of the period with lists of individual titles including composer, lyricist, artist, and publication or recording information.

Chapter 3: Cataloging

THEMATIC INDEXES

Barlow, Harold, and Sam Morgenstern. *A Dictionary of Musical Themes*. Rev. ed. New York: Crown, 1975. Themes are arranged alphabetically by composer, then by title. The Notation Index is used to identify the work by its opening melodic pitches, using a system devised by Barlow. A title index is included at the back of the book. Available online as The Electronic Dictionary of Musical Themes (http://www.multimedialibrary.com/barlow/index.asp).

———. *A Dictionary of Opera and Song Themes, Including Cantatas, Oratorios, Lieder and Art Songs*. Rev. ed. New York: Crown, 1976. Themes are arranged alphabetically by composer, then by title. Many modern works are omitted (e.g., *Elektra, Salome*). An index to song titles and first lines appears in the back of the book.

Brook, Barry, and Richard Viano. *Thematic Catalogues in Music: An Annotated Bibliography*. Stuyvesant, N.Y.: Pendragon Press, 1997. Contains bibliographic citations for more than 1,500 thematic catalogs of composers, arranged alphabetically by name, then library location, publisher, compiler or author. Indexes to name, subject, title, genre, compiler, and author are included.

Burrows, Raymond, and Bessie Carroll Redmond. *Concerto Themes*. New York: Simon and Schuster, 1951.

———. *Symphony Themes*. New York: Simon and Schuster, 1942. In addition to musical incipits of major themes, each entry includes publication information for scores, program note and analysis citations, and a discography. There are indexes by keys, titles, and concerto solo instrument, but not by the musical themes themselves.

Parsons, Denys. *The Directory of Tunes and Musical Themes*. Cambridge, England: Spencer Brown, 1975. International ed. Lubeck, Germany: Bohmeier Verlag, 2002. Includes classical themes as well as popular songs (movie themes, etc.) and national anthems. This thematic notation system (sometimes called the up-down method) is easier to use than Barlow's system (mentioned above).

DICTIONARIES AND TERMINOLOGY GUIDES

Ammer, Christine. *The A to Z of Foreign Musical Terms*. Boston, Mass.: ECS Publishing, 1989. A handy, portable dictionary, containing many terms found in orchestral and ensemble music.

Boccagna, David. *Musical Terminology: A Practical Compendium in Four Languages*. Stuyvestant, N.Y.: Pendragon Press, 1999. Arranged by language (Italian, French, German, English), the entries show the corresponding terms in the other languages, but give no actual definitions.

Del Mar, Norman. *Anatomy of the Orchestra*. Rev. ed. Berkeley: University of California Press, 1983. Del Mar describes the instruments and explains their individual and ensemble functions within the symphony orchestra, with notes on uncommon performance practice, notation, and terms found in the orchestral literature.

———. *A Companion to the Orchestra*. London: Faber and Faber, 1987. Contains information about instruments, terminology, and the activities of the symphony orchestra, arranged in a dictionary format. Also published as *The Anchor Companion to the Orchestra* (Garden City, N.Y.: Anchor Press, 1987).

Grigg, Carolyn Doub. *Music Translation Dictionary: An English, Czech, Danish, Dutch, French, German, Hungarian, Italian, Polish, Portuguese, Russian, Spanish, Swedish Vocabulary of Musical Terms*. Westport, Conn.: Greenwood Press, 1978. A list of musical terms and instruments with English as the basic language. There is a complete index to all words in all languages and a separate index for terms in the Cyrillic alphabet.

Katzyen, Lelia, and Val Telberg. *Russian-English Dictionary of Musical Terms*. New York: Telberg Book Corp., 1965. Includes terms that appeared regularly in Russian materials between 1945 and 1964. Untranslatable terms are transliterated into English. Arranged according to the Cyrillic alphabet, it does not include a corresponding English to Russian section.

Leuchtmann, Horst. *Wörterbuch Music: Dictionary of Terms in Music. (English–German/German–English)*. 5th ed. Stuttgart: J. B. Metzler, 1998. A detailed German translation dictionary also containing many abbreviations and acronyms. The appendix features an illustrated guide to music notation in both languages.

Leuchtmann, Horst, editor-in-chief. *Teminorum Musicae Index Septum Linguis Redactus—Polyglot Dictionary of Musical Terms: English, German, French, Italian, Spanish, Hungarian, Russian*. Kassel: Bärenreiter; Budapest: Akadémiai Kiadó, 1978. Terms are arranged in alphabetical order using German as the basic language. There are no definitions, but each term shows the translation into the five other languages. There is a separate glossary for the Cyrillic alphabet and an appendix with forty-four diagrams identifying elements of music notation and parts of musical instruments in each language.

Moore, Shirley. *A French-English Music Dictionary*. Atlanta, Ga.: Leihall Publications, 1985. This one-way (French to English only) dictionary translates over 4,000 musical terms, phrases, and titles, geared toward players and conductors. Pronunciation is given for most entries.

Chapter 5: Part Preparation

BOWINGS

A bibliography on bowing manuals and instruction is listed in the article "Music Preparation: How to Mark Parts."

ERRATA SOURCES

A bibliography on errata resources is listed in the article "Errata."

MUSIC NOTATION MANUALS

A bibliography of notation manuals is listed in the article "Music Notation Guidelines."

ORCHESTRAL EXCERPTS AND AUDITION MATERIAL

Akos, Katherine, Marshall Burlingame, and Jack Wellbaum, compilers and editors. *Facing the Maestro: A Musician's Guide to Orchestral Audition Repertoire*. Washington, D.C.: American Symphony Orchestra League, 1983. Contains lists of the most requested audition repertoire by instrument, frequency of request, and composer. Includes publisher addresses and music sources.

Rabson, Carolyn. *Orchestral Excerpts: A Comprehensive Index*. Berkeley, Calif.: Fallen Leaf Press, 1993. An index of published collections of excerpts and parts for orchestral instruments.

PERCUSSION ASSIGNMENT BOOKS

These manuals provide percussion player assignments and instruments required for orchestral and wind ensemble music. While they may differ in the number and distribution of players and instruments, they are useful to librarians, personnel managers, and section leaders to help determine staffing and equipment needs. An index to the orchestral manuals is located at http://www.mola-inc.org/pdf/PercussionAssignments.pdf.

Carroll, Raynor. *Symphonic Repertoire Guide for Timpani and Percussion*. Pasadena, Calif.: Batterie Music [distributed by Carl Fischer], 2005.

Cotton, Maggie. *Percussion Work Book*. 3rd ed. Birmingham, England: Maggie Cotton, 1993.

Girsberger, Russ. *Percussion Assignments for Band & Wind Ensemble*. Fort Lauderdale, Fla.: Meredith Music Publications, 2004. 2 volumes.

Holmstrand, Bo. *Percussion Instrumentation Guide for Symphony Orchestra.* [Gothenburg, Sweden]: Edition Excobar, 2004.

Huber, Horst. *Pauke und Schlagzeug in den Werken von Haydn bis Messiaen.* [Munich: the author, 2003.]

de Vlieger, Henk. *Handbook for the Orchestral Percussion Section.* The Hague, the Netherlands: Albersen, 2003.

INDEX

Text in **bold** type identifies an illustration.

A

accession numbers. *See* shelf
  arrangement
accordion-fold parts. *See* binding music
acid-free. *See* preservation materials
acquisitions
  band music, 27
  bibliography, 40–43, 184–187
  choral music, 20, 27
  educational institutions, 25
  lending libraries and consortiums, 25
  music for sale, 8–9
  online and digital resources, 26–27
  ordering music, 9
  other sources, 25–27
  purchasing music, 20–21
  receiving music, 30–31
  rental music, 7–8
  schedule, 20–23, 28
  See also editions
acquisitions record keeping, 21, 28–31,
    125
  active files, 29
  historical files, 29
arranging materials on shelves. *See* shelf
    arrangement
ASCAP. *See* performing
    rights—organizations
auditions
  access to audition material, 144
  audition lists, 142–145, **145**
  bibliography, 189
  excerpts, 146–149, **148–149**
authority sources. *See* cataloging–
    authority sources

B

band and wind ensemble
  acquisitions. *See* acquisitions—band
      music
  bibliography, 41, 186
  march-size music, 3, 52–53, 73,
      110–113
  numbering parts, 68
  score order, 63–65
band instrument substitutions, 160
bibliographies of music, 184–187
big band. *See* jazz ensemble
binding music, 99–102, **100–101**
  score binding, 102, 133
  See also supplies—binding supplies
BMI. *See* performing
    rights—organizations
bowings
  bibliography, 80
  bow marker assignment form, **173**
  bowing box, 14
  cleaning parts, 76–78, **77, 79**, 124
  divisi markings, **81–84**
  See also supplies
budget, 28

C

career information, 183–184
catalog 2, 4, 34–36
  format, 34
cataloging
  authority sources, 34, 37–39, 53
  bibliography and resources, 40–43,
      56–58, 187–189
  cleaning the database, 35–36
  copy cataloging, 42–43
  data entry format, 34–35
  excerpts from a larger work, 38
  forms, **162–169**
  information to include, 34
  initial articles, 38–39
  language choice, 39
  names, 37, 40, 42
  online resources, 42–43
  score identification, 44–51
  subject headings, 55–58
  thesaurus, 55–56, 58
  titles, 37–39, 42

chamber music
    bibliography, 186–187
choral music, 27
    acquisitions. *See* acquisitions—choral
        music
    bibliography, 41, 186
    numbering parts, 69
    shelf arrangement, 3
composers
    bibliography, 135–136
    student composers, 130–136
concert folders, 17
    booking folders, 118
    breaking down folders, 123
concert procedures, 119–121
    collecting music, 121, 122
    putting away concert music, 126
conductors
    bibliography, 140–141
    interaction with, 9
    student conductors, 137–141
copyright, 7
customer service. *See* professionalism
cuts, **86–87**

D

dance band. *See* jazz ensemble
dictionaries and terminology guides
    bibliography, 188–189

E

editions, 9, 20, 138–139, 141, 142–143
    definition, 6
equipment and supplies. *See* supplies
errata, 20, 150–159
    bibliography, 151–153
    MOLA errata forms, 154–159, **158–159**
etiquette, 10–11

F

files. *See* office and administrative files
filing systems. *See* shelf arrangement—
    filing systems

film and theater music
    bibliography, 42, 185–186
folders. *See* concert folders. *See*
    supplies—music folders
forms, 5, 161–174
    bowing assignments, **173**
    cataloging, **162–169**
    errata **158–159**
    inventory sheet, 35, **70, 165–169**
    music preparation, **170–172**
    performance record, **71, 174**

G

GATT Treaty (General Agreement on
    Tariffs and Trade), 7, 185

H

hire music. *See* rental music

I

inventory forms, 4, **70, 165–169**
inventory of library holdings, 4

J

jazz ensemble
    cataloging form, **169**
    score order, 65
jazz music
    bibliography, 42

L

library manuals and practices
    bibliography, 182–183

M

Major Orchestra Librarians' Association
    (MOLA), 12, 20, 53, 97, 135, 141,
    150–152, 154–159 182, 184
march-size music. *See* band and wind
    ensemble—march-size music
measure numbers. *See* rehearsal
    figures—measure numbers

MOLA. *See* Major Orchestra
   Librarians' Association
music dealers, 9, 26, 138
music folders. *See* supplies—music
   folders
music storage. *See* supplies—music
   storage
musical theater. *See* film and theater
   music
mutes
   terminology, 85

N

notation, **77**, **93–96**, 93–98, 130
   bibliography, 97–98, 135–136
numbering measures. *See* rehearsal
   figures—measure numbers
numbering parts, 31, 67–69
   band and wind ensemble, 68
   choir, 69
   orchestra, 67–68
   scores, 69

O

office and administrative files, 5, 28–29
opera
   bibliography, 41–42, 185–186
orchestra
   bibliography, 26–27, 40, 185
   numbering parts, 67–68
   score order, 62–63

P

page turns, 8, 16, 86, 99, 101, **103–108**,
   130, 132, 141
paper. *See* supplies—paper
part preparation, 76–92, 99–115
   format, **131–132**
   music preparation form, **170–172**
   percussion parts, **131**
percussion instruments, 62–65, 68, 98,
   133, 136
   substitutions, 160

percussion part assignments, 68
   bibliography, 189–190
percussion parts. *See* part preparation–
   percussion parts
performance aids, **85**
   instrument changes, 85
performance record, 6, **71**, 120, 126,
   174
performing rights, 22, 183
   licenses, 23
   organizations (ASCAP, BMI,
      SOCAN), 7, 23
photocopying, 109
   march-size music, 110–113, **111–112**
popular music
   bibliography, 42, 187
preservation materials
   supplies, 3, 15, 17, 73
preservation set, 72–73, 110
professionalism, 10–11, 76
   bibliography, 11
   career information bibliography,
      183–184
   library manuals and practices,
      182–183
   online resources, 182
program planning, 6–9
   scheduling, 20–21
property markings, **66**, 113
public domain, 7–8, 26, 27, 144
   definition, 7
publishers, 9, 22, 26, 72, 99, 119, 124–
   125, 133, 138, 143–144
   rental form, **24**
   reprint publishers, 7, 8, 73; definition, 8

R

rehearsal figures, 6, 9, 13, 31, 34,
   88–92, 131, 138, 139, 155
   counting measures, 91–**92**,
   crib sheet, 92
   endings, **91**
   measure numbers, **90–92**

rental music, 7–8, 22–24, 28–29, 31, 71, 78, 99, 108
   on-deposit sets, 7
   quotes, 22
   returning, 124–125
   See also acquisitions—rental music
reprint publishers. *See* publishers—reprint publishers

S

scheduling, 20–21, 22–23
score order, 45, 62–65, 67, 118, 121–124
   band and wind ensemble, 63–65
   choir, 69
   jazz ensemble, 65
   orchestra, 62–63
scores, 20, 119–121
   binding, 16, 102
   cataloging, 44–51
   format, **44–45**, 90, 97, 133
   numbering, 69
   storage and shelf arrangement, 4, 52–53
SESAC. *See* performing rights organizations
shelf arrangement 2–4, 52–53
   filing systems, 52–54
   scores. *See* scores—storage and shelf arrangement
SOCAN. *See* performing rights organizations

special collections, 3, 53
   preservation set, 72–73
stage band. *See* jazz ensemble
storage materials. *See* supplies—music storage
student conductors. *See* conductors—student conductors
supplies, 4, 12–17
   adhesive tape, 14–15
   adhesives, 14
   binding supplies, 15–16, 99
   bowing box, 14
   bowing pencils, 12
   correction tape and fluid, 14
   envelopes, 16, 73
   erasers, 13
   music cart, 119
   music folders, 17
   music storage, 16–17
   paper, 16
   pens, 13, 93
   preservation. *See* preservation materials—supplies
   rulers and drafting templates, 13, 93
   traveling concert supplies, 119, 121

T

thematic indexes, 187–188

W

wind ensemble. *See* band and wind ensemble

ABOUT THE AUTHORS

RUSS GIRSBERGER is the Ensemble Librarian at The Juilliard School in New York City. He has worked as a performance librarian with the New England Conservatory, the Boston Symphony and Boston Pops, the New York Philharmonic, and the United States Marine Band. Girsberger holds degrees in music education, music history, and library and information science. He is the author of *A Manual for the Performance Library, Percussion Assignments for Band & Wind Ensemble,* and *A Practical Guide to Percussion Terminology*.

LAURIE LAKE holds a BM in music performance from Northwestern University and an MLS from Indiana University. She performed as a flutist in the Honolulu Symphony where she was also the orchestra's librarian. She has managed the libraries for the Aspen Music Festival and School, as well as run the ensemble libraries at Indiana University and the Interlochen Center for the Arts. Ms Lake served the Major Orchestra Librarians' Association (MOLA) as their first president from an educational institution. She is currently the Reference and Electronic Resources Librarian at the Cleveland Institute of Music's Robinson Music Library.

INSIGHTS AND ESSAYS ON THE MUSIC PERFORMANCE LIBRARY,

edited by Russ Girsberger and Laurie Lake • ISBN 978-1-57463-176-0

The music performance library is the heart of a musical ensemble, supplying music to performers and information to an entire organization. There is valuable information here for all musicians—music directors, conductors, student librarians, community volunteers, and professional performance librarians—written by musicians from today's premier organizations:

- Alabama Symphony
- Boosey & Hawkes
- Boston Symphony Orchestra
- Cleveland Orchestra
- Dallas Symphony Orchestra
- European American Music
- Finnish Music Information Centre
- Florida Orchestra
- Fort Worth Symphony Orchestra
- Glimmerglass Opera
- Indianapolis Symphony Orchestra
- Interlochen Center for the Arts
- Jazz at Lincoln Center
- Juilliard School
- Kansas City Symphony
- Los Angeles Philharmonic

- McGill University
- Metropolitan Opera
- Milwaukee Symphony
- Minnesota Orchestra
- National Symphony Orchestra
- New England Conservatory
- New York Philharmonic
- Minnesota Orchestra
- Philadelphia Orchestra
- San Diego Symphony
- San Francisco Ballet
- San Francisco Symphony
- Seattle Symphony Orchestra
- United States Army Field Band
- United States Marine Band
- United States Military Academy Band

———•◆•———

"With anecdotes and nuggets of essential recommendations, the book is not only a musical survival kit, but also a true pleasure to read. This is a valuable tool that ought to be on the desk of everyone in the field of orchestral music, including composers, conductor, orchestra managers and recording engineers."

— **JOHN ADAMS, Composer, Conductor, Author**

"It's an excellent overview of all aspects of music ensemble librarianship, with advice and insights from the foremost experts in the field."

— **JANE GOTTLIEB, Vice President of Library and Information Resources, The Juilliard School**